GAME-DAY
Fan Fare

Gooseberry Patch
2500 Farmers Dr., #110
Columbus, OH 43235

www.gooseberrypatch.com

1·800·854·6673

Copyright 2012, Gooseberry Patch 978-1-62093-015-1
Second Printing, August, 2013

Do you have a tried & true recipe...

tip, craft or memory that you'd like to see featured in a **Gooseberry Patch** cookbook? Visit our website at **www.gooseberrypatch.com** to share them with us instantly. If you'd rather jot them down by hand, use the handy form in the front of this book and send them to...

Gooseberry Patch
Attn: Cookbook Dept.
2500 Farmers Dr., #110
Columbus, OH 43235

Don't forget to include the number of servings your recipe makes, plus your name, address, phone number and email address. If we select your recipe, your name will appear right along with it...and you'll receive a **FREE** copy of the cookbook!

Contents

Kick-Off Brunches 5

Major League Munchies 35

Souper-Bowl Soups,
Salads & Sandwiches 75

Slam-Dunk Mains
& Sides 107

Touchdown Treats 147

Stadium-Sized Recipes
for a Crowd 183

Dedication

For everyone who loves getting together with family, friends and great food just as much as watching the big game!

Appreciation

A big thank-you to all the tailgating party pros who sent us their best game-day dishes...we couldn't have done it without you!

KICK-OFF
Brunches

Goal-Line Sausage Casserole

Staci Prickett
Montezuma, GA

This is a great recipe to make the night before a big day. Just pop it in the oven the next morning. Try different flavor combinations like spicy sausage and Pepper Jack cheese or Italian sausage and mozzarella cheese...the choices are endless!

6 slices bread, cubed
1 lb. ground pork breakfast
   sausage, browned and
   drained
8-oz. pkg. shredded Cheddar
   cheese

6 to 8 eggs
2 c. milk
1 t. dry mustard

Evenly spread bread cubes in a lightly greased 13"x9" baking pan. Top bread with sausage; sprinkle with cheese. In a bowl, beat together eggs, milk and mustard. Pour over cheese. Cover with aluminum foil and refrigerate overnight. Bake, uncovered, at 350 degrees for 45 minutes, or until set and top is golden. Serves 6 to 8.

The two most important things in life
are good friends and a strong bullpen.

–Bob Lemon

Mrs. V's Southwest Quiche

Jamie Volner
Tucson, AZ

I have to admit I am very picky about my quiche. So, many moons ago, not even knowing how to make a quiche, I practiced, flopped and failed until I created this one. It became an instant hit with the family!

9-inch deep-dish pie crust
8 slices bacon, chopped
4 green onions, chopped
1 c. shredded Swiss cheese,
   divided
1 c. shredded Pepper Jack cheese,
   divided

6 eggs
1 c. whipping cream
1/2 t. salt
1/8 t. white pepper
1/8 t. cayenne pepper
1/2 t. nutmeg

Place crust in a 9" pie plate; pierce bottom and sides of crust several times with a fork. Bake at 400 degrees for 5 minutes. Remove from oven and set aside. Cook bacon in a skillet over medium heat until crisp; drain on paper towels. Combine bacon, onions and half of cheeses in crust. In a bowl, beat together eggs, cream and seasonings. Pour over mixture in crust. Sprinkle with remaining cheeses and nutmeg. Bake at 350 degrees for 50 minutes to one hour, until a toothpick inserted in the center tests clean. If edge of crust browns too quickly, cover with strips of aluminum foil. Let cool 10 minutes before slicing. Cut into wedges to serve. Serves 6.

Bite-size treats always disappear fast at a potluck and are a snap to make. Simply bake a favorite quiche in mini muffin pans...just reduce the baking time by about 10 minutes!

Pumpkin Pancakes & Waffles

Karla Visser
Pella, IA

My husband loves pumpkin, so I have been on the search for dishes to create with pumpkin. He's especially fond of this tasty recipe!

2 c. biscuit baking mix
1/4 c. sugar
2 t. cinnamon
1 t. pumpkin pie spice

5-oz. can evaporated milk
2 T. oil
1 t. vanilla extract
15-oz. can pumpkin

In a bowl, combine baking mix, sugar and spices. In a separate bowl, combine remaining ingredients. Pour into dry ingredients; mix well. For pancakes, pour batter by 1/3 cupfuls onto a lightly greased hot griddle over medium heat. When bubbles start to form on tops, flip and cook other side until golden. For waffles, pour batter by 1/3 cupfuls into a lightly greased waffle iron. Cook according to manufacturer's instructions. Makes about one dozen pancakes or waffles.

Peanut Butter Pancake Syrup

Cyndy DeStefano
Mercer, PA

While vacationing in the South, we enjoyed this tasty treat at a small hometown diner. My version is close to the original... it's simple and oh-so yummy!

1/2 c. maple syrup

1/4 c. creamy peanut butter

Combine syrup and peanut butter in a saucepan over medium heat. Stir and cook until hot and well blended. Makes 4 servings.

KICK-OFF *Brunches*

Reuben Quiche

Samantha Starks
Madison, WI

I've always loved Reuben sandwiches. So one morning when I was craving one but the deli wasn't open yet, I decided to try and make a Reuben quiche. I was amazed how tasty it turned out. Now I can enjoy my favorite sandwich any time of day!

5 slices rye bread, toasted and
   crumbled
4 T. butter, melted and divided
4 green onions, chopped
1-1/2 c. shredded Swiss cheese,
   divided
1/4 lb. deli corned beef, chopped

1/2 c. sauerkraut, well drained
4 eggs, beaten
1 c. half-and-half
1 T. all-purpose flour
1 T. Dijon mustard
Optional: dill pickle slices

Toss bread crumbs with 3 tablespoons melted butter; pat into the bottom and up the sides of a 9" pie plate. Bake at 375 degrees for 5 to 7 minutes, until lightly golden. Remove from oven and set aside. Meanwhile, in a skillet over medium heat, sauté onions in remaining butter until tender; drain and set aside. Top crust with 1/2 cup cheese, corned beef and sauerkraut. Sprinkle with remaining cheese. In a bowl, beat together eggs, half-and-half, flour, onion mixture and mustard; pour into crust. Bake at 375 degrees for 25 to 30 minutes, until a knife tip inserted in center tests clean. Let stand several minutes before slicing into wedges. Garnish with pickles, if desired. Serves 6 to 8.

Serve breakfast juices in glasses with a bit of sparkle. Run a lemon wedge around the rims of glasses, then dip rims in superfine sugar. Garnish each with a sprig of fresh mint.

Cheesy Chicken Omelet

Paulette Alexander
Newfoundland, Canada

This is a nice switch from everyday omelets. My son just loves it!
It's even better with fruit and yogurt on the side.

2 slices bacon, chopped
1 t. butter
1 T. green pepper, chopped
1 green onion, chopped
1 clove garlic, minced
3 eggs
salt and pepper to taste

2 T. cooked chicken, chopped
1 T. ranch salad dressing
1-1/2 T. tomato, chopped
1/2 c. shredded Cheddar cheese
1/4 c. shredded mozzarella
  cheese

Cook bacon in a skillet over medium heat until crisp; drain and set
aside. Melt butter in skillet over medium heat. Sauté green pepper,
onion and garlic until crisp-tender. In a bowl, beat together eggs, salt
and pepper; pour over vegetables in skillet and cover. In a small bowl,
mix together bacon, chicken and salad dressing. When omelet is almost
set, flip and spread bacon mixture over top. Sprinkle with tomato and
cheeses. Remove from heat and let stand, covered, until cheeses are
melted. Fold over and cut in half before serving. Serves 2.

Want fresh orange juice but don't have a juicer? No worries,
just use a pair of kitchen tongs! While holding the tongs closed,
stick the tips of the tongs into a halved orange and twist to juice.

Migas

Eliza Salinas
Kingsville, TX

This scrumptious Tex-Mex staple is so versatile and a great way to use up bits and pieces of tortillas. You can add bacon, ham, cheese, jalapeños, asparagus...just about anything!

6 6-inch corn tortillas
2 t. oil
1/2 onion, chopped
1 tomato, chopped

6 eggs
salt and pepper to taste
2 to 3 t. tomato sauce

Tear tortillas into bite-size pieces. Heat oil in a large skillet over medium-high heat. Fry tortilla pieces in oil until crisp. Add onion and cook one minute; stir in tomato. In a bowl, beat together eggs, salt and pepper; pour over ingredients in skillet. Cook and stir until eggs are set. Remove skillet from heat and top with tomato sauce. Serves 4 to 6.

Watch yard sales for a vintage salad dressing server... it's just as handy for serving up salsa, guacamole and sour cream for Tex-Mex dishes!

Mama's Camping Burritos

Yvette Garza
Livingston, CA

We eat these scrumptious and filling burritos every time we go camping. They always hit the spot. By prepping some ingredients the night before, cooking the next morning is a breeze.

1 lb. bacon, crisply cooked and
   crumbled
2 30-oz. pkgs. frozen shredded
   hashbrowns, thawed
2 onions, chopped
1 c. butter, sliced
2 1-oz. pkgs. onion soup mix

18 eggs, beaten
8-oz. pkg. shredded Mexican-
   blend cheese
12 10-inch flour tortillas
Garnish: chopped onion, chopped
   fresh cilantro, salsa

In a large bowl, combine bacon, hashbrowns, onions, butter and soup mix; cover and refrigerate overnight. In the morning, transfer bacon mixture to a very large skillet over medium heat. Cook, stirring occasionally, for 10 to 15 minutes, until golden. Pour eggs over hashbrown mixture. Cook and stir until eggs reach desired consistency. Warm tortillas according to package directions. Divide hashbrown mixture and cheese evenly among tortillas. Garnish as desired. Roll up burritos before serving. Makes 10 to 12 burritos.

Make extra burritos and freeze them for an easy heat & eat meal later! Wrap each cooled burrito in plastic wrap, then in aluminum foil. Place wrapped burritos in a freezer-safe zipping bag marked with the date...so simple!

Slow-Cooker Piggies in Eggs

Betty Stewart
Paducah, KY

I often take this casserole to Sunday school. I make sure to double the ingredients, because it's always a huge hit!

6 eggs, beaten
14-oz. pkg. mini smoked
   sausages
1-1/2 c. milk
1 c. shredded Cheddar cheese

8 slices bread, torn
1 t. salt
1/2 t. dry mustard
1 c. shredded mozzarella cheese

In a bowl, combine all ingredients except mozzarella cheese. Pour into a lightly greased slow cooker. Sprinkle mozzarella cheese over top. Cover and cook on high setting for 2 hours, then on low setting for one hour. Serves 8 to 10.

Skillet Crumb Cake

Angel Lumbatis
Lewisville, OH

This cake can be baked the day before and reheated in the oven on low heat the next day. It's a great game-day morning treat!

1/3 c. shortening
3/4 c. sugar
2 eggs
1-3/4 c. self-rising flour
3/4 c. milk

1/3 c. chopped nuts
2 T. all-purpose flour
1/2 c. brown sugar, packed
1 t. cinnamon
2 T. butter, softened

Lightly grease and flour a 10" cast-iron skillet; set aside. In a bowl, beat together shortening and sugar until fluffy. Beat in eggs, one at a time. Alternately mix in flour and milk. Fold in nuts; pour into skillet. In a bowl, mix together remaining ingredients until crumbly. Sprinkle over batter in skillet. Bake at 375 for 35 minutes, or until a toothpick inserted in the center tests clean. Cut into wedges to serve. Serves 6 to 8.

Ham & Corn Griddle Cakes

Zoe Bennett
Columbia, SC

I had some leftover ham and corn from the previous night's dinner, so I thought I might try using them up for breakfast the next day. With a little creativity and trial & error, I came up with these scrumptious griddle cakes.

1-1/3 c. all-purpose flour
1/2 c. yellow cornmeal
1 T. baking powder
2 T. sugar
2 t. salt
2 eggs, beaten
1/2 c. milk

2 T. oil
15-oz. can creamed corn
1 c. corn
1 c. cooked ham, finely diced
oil for frying
Garnish: cinnamon applesauce
Optional: powdered sugar

In a large bowl, stir together flour, cornmeal, baking powder, sugar and salt. In a separate bowl, combine eggs, milk, oil and creamed corn. Add egg mixture to flour mixture; stir well. Fold in corn and ham. Heat 1/2 inch oil in a large skillet over medium heat. For each griddle cake, ladle 1/2 cup of batter into hot oil. Cook until edges are dry and bottom is golden. Flip and cook other side until golden. Serve griddlecakes with warm applesauce and a dusting of powdered sugar, if desired. Serves 3 to 6.

Mix pancake or waffle batter in a wide-mouth, spouted pitcher, then pour right onto the griddle...less dishes to wash!

Beer Bread Pancakes

Claire Bertram
Lexington, KY

If you like the sweet taste of beer bread, then you're going to love these pancakes. They're oh-so good topped with a big pat of butter and a generous drizzle of maple syrup.

1-3/4 c. all-purpose flour
1-1/2 t. baking powder
1/2 t. baking soda
1/2 t. salt
1 egg, beaten

3 T. oil
1 T. molasses
12-oz. bottle beer or
    non-alcoholic beer

In a bowl, combine flour, baking powder, baking soda and salt. In a separate bowl, combine egg, oil and molasses. Add egg mixture to flour mixture; slowly pour in beer. Stir well to combine. Batter will be thick and slightly lumpy. Spoon batter by 1/4 cupfuls onto a lightly greased griddle over medium-high heat. Spread batter on griddle with the back of the spoon to about 3-inch rounds. Cook until bottom is golden, about 3 to 4 minutes. Flip and cook until other side is golden. Serves 4.

Yummy pancake & waffle topping in your favorite fruit flavor!
Combine a small box of fruit-flavored gelatin, one cup water,
1/2 cup sugar and 2 tablespoons cornstarch in a saucepan.
Bring to a rolling boil; pour into a syrup pitcher and
let cool slightly before serving.

Michigan Game-Day Oatmeal

Pat Rompa
Waterford, MI

*This hearty baked oatmeal will warm anyone up on
a chilly morning before the big game.*

2 c. long-cooking oats, uncooked
4 c. milk
1/2 t. almond extract
1/4 c. brown sugar, packed

1/2 c. sliced almonds
1/2 c. dried cherries
1 Granny Smith apple, cored and
   grated

In a bowl, mix together all ingredients. Pour into a lightly greased
13"x9" baking pan. Bake, uncovered, at 400 degrees for 45 minutes.
Serves 6.

Baked Denver Omelet

Donna Lewis
Ostrander, OH

*These tasty omelets are a breakfast staple. They're simple to
toss together, and nothing compares to the taste of
a Denver omelet on a sunny morning.*

8 eggs
1 c. milk
1/2 t. seasoned salt
2 c. frozen shredded
   hashbrowns, thawed

1 c. cooked ham, diced
1 c. shredded Cheddar cheese
1 T. onion, minced

In a bowl, beat together eggs, milk and salt. Stir in remaining
ingredients until well mixed. Pour into a greased 8"x8" baking pan.
Bake, uncovered, at 350 degrees for 45 to 50 minutes, until a knife
inserted near the center tests clean. Serves 4.

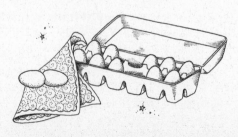

Chocolate Chip Banana Pancakes
Jennifer Hathcock
Temple, GA

I love love love chocolate chip banana muffins, so I decided to experiment and try them as pancakes. These are a hit with my son and husband!

2 bananas
1 c. biscuit baking mix
1/2 to 3/4 c. water

1/2 c. semi-sweet chocolate chips
Garnish: maple syrup
Optional: whipped cream

Mash bananas in a bowl. Add baking mix to bananas; pour in 1/2 cup water. Mix well, adding more water if necessary for batter to reach desired consistency. Fold in chocolate chips. Pour batter by 1/4 cupfuls onto a lightly greased hot griddle. Cook over medium heat until bubbly on top; flip and continue to cook until golden. Top with maple syrup and whipped cream, if desired. Makes 6 to 7 pancakes.

Leftover pancakes are easy to store and reheat. Just freeze pancakes in plastic freezer zipping bags. To reheat, place pancakes in a single layer on baking sheets. Bake at 350 degrees for 5 to 10 minutes, then they're ready to be topped!

Jumbo Cinnamon Rolls

Darlene Hartzler
Marshallville, OH

These classic cinnamon rolls are perfect for a get-together before the big game. The heavenly aroma of these rolls baking in the oven will have your guests' mouths watering!

1 T. active dry yeast
1/4 c. warm water
1/4 c. instant vanilla pudding
   mix
1 c. milk
1/4 c. oil
1 egg, beaten

4 c. all-purpose flour
2 T. sugar
1/2 t. salt
1-1/2 T. cinnamon
1/2 c. brown sugar, packed
16-oz. can vanilla frosting

In a large bowl, dissolve yeast in very warm water, about 110 to 115 degrees. In a separate bowl, combine dry pudding mix, milk, oil and egg. Add pudding mixture to yeast mixture. In another bowl, sift together flour, sugar and salt. Add pudding mixture to flour mixture; stir until mixed well and dough forms. Transfer dough to a lightly floured surface; knead for 4 minutes. Place in a greased bowl; let rise, covered, for one hour. Meanwhile, combine cinnamon and brown sugar in a bowl. Roll dough out into a 13-inch by 10-inch rectangle; evenly sprinkle with cinnamon mixture. Roll up dough, starting at a long edge; slice into 12 to 15 rolls. Let rolls rise until double in bulk, about one hour. Transfer rolls to lightly greased baking sheets and bake at 350 degrees for about 15 minutes, until golden. Spread each roll with frosting. Makes 12 to 15 rolls.

Whip up some creamy homemade vanilla frosting in no time. Beat together 1/3 c. butter, 3 cups powdered sugar, 1-1/2 teaspoons vanilla extract and 2 tablespoons milk. This makes the yummiest frosting for spreading on Jumbo Cinnamon Rolls.

Fresh Spinach Quiche

Sharon Lundberg
Longwood, FL

We usually eat quiches for breakfast or brunch, but my family loves
this savory quiche for dinner too. I like to bake two, and then
we have the leftovers for breakfast throughout the week.

2 T. onion, chopped
1 T. butter
4 eggs
1 c. milk
1/2 c. shredded sharp Cheddar
    cheese

1/2 c. shredded white Cheddar
    cheese
3/4 c. fresh spinach
9-inch pie crust

In a skillet over medium heat, sauté onion in butter until translucent;
set aside. In a large bowl, beat together eggs and milk. Stir in cheeses,
spinach and onion mixture. Pour egg mixture into crust. Bake at
350 degrees for 50 minutes, or until a knife tip inserted near the center
tests clean. Cut into wedges. Serves 6.

Keep salad greens farmstand-fresh for up to a week. After you
bring them home, rinse greens in cool water, wrap in paper
towels and slip into a plastic zipping bag with several small
holes cut in it. Tuck the bag in the fridge's crisper bin...
ready to serve when you are!

Sausage & Grits Casserole

Arlene Grimm
Decatur, AL

I got this recipe from a dear friend, and it's so versatile. Add some of your favorite vegetables, use a different type of cheese, or add ham or bacon instead of sausage...it's delicious no matter what!

1 lb. spicy ground pork breakfast
    sausage
1/2 c. onion, finely chopped
1 c. quick-cooking grits,
    uncooked
2-1/4 c. shredded sharp Cheddar
    cheese, divided

3 eggs, beaten
2 T. butter
1-1/2 T. milk
1/2 t. salt
1/4 t. pepper

Brown sausage and onion in a large skillet over medium heat; drain and set aside. Cook grits according to package directions. In a bowl, combine sausage mixture, grits, 2 cups cheese and remaining ingredients; mix well. Pour into a greased 13"x9" baking pan; cover loosely with aluminum foil. Bake at 350 degrees for 50 to 55 minutes. Remove foil and sprinkle with remaining cheese. Let stand until cheese melts, about 2 to 3 minutes. Serves 8 to 10.

Take brunch outdoors! Spread out a quilt on the picnic table, gather everyone 'round and enjoy the warm, sunny weather.

Cannoli French Toast

Jackie Maechtle
Kewaskum, WI

I love to add mini chocolate chips to the ricotta mixture for an extra-sweet surprise. We always make this recipe when our family vacations together.

1/4 c. powdered sugar
1 c. ricotta cheese
Optional: 1/4 c. mini semi-sweet
  chocolate chips
2 eggs
1/2 c. milk

12 slices white bread, crusts
  trimmed
2 T. oil
Garnish: additional powdered
  sugar, chocolate syrup

Sift sugar into a bowl; stir in ricotta cheese and chocolate chips, if using. In a separate bowl, beat together eggs and milk; set aside. Using a rolling pin, flatten each slice of bread. Add about one tablespoon ricotta mixture to each bread slice. Fold over bread and pinch edges together to seal. Heat oil in a large skillet over medium heat. Dip each stuffed bread slice into egg mixture. Fry bread slices, 3 at a time, in oil until puffed and golden, turning once. Dust with powdered sugar and drizzle with chocolate syrup before serving. Serves 6.

A great gift for Dad! Wake him up with some Cannoli French Toast and a coupon good for an indoor tailgating party...uninterrupted football coverage complete with his favorite snacks and drinks.

Line-Drive Doughnuts

Georgia Medsker
Caney, KS

When I was a little girl, my mom would get together with her lady friends and make these doughnuts to sell at bake sales. I still remember the heavenly smell and delicious taste when I got to try one!

1 env. active dry yeast
1 T. sugar
1/4 c. warm water, about
    110 to 115 degrees
1 c. warm milk
3 T. butter, softened

1/4 c. sugar
1 t. salt
1 egg, beaten
3-1/2 c. all-purpose flour
oil for deep frying

In a large bowl, combine yeast, sugar and warm water; let stand 10 minutes. Add milk and remaining ingredients except oil; mix until a smooth dough forms. Cover and let rise until double in size, about one hour. Roll out dough 1/2-inch thick; cut with a doughnut cutter. Let rise 15 minutes. In a deep saucepan, heat several inches of oil to 350 degrees. Fry doughnuts, a few at a time, flipping once, until golden. Dip in Glaze while warm; cool on wax paper. Makes 3 dozen.

Glaze:

1/2 c. milk
2 T. butter
16-oz. pkg. powdered sugar

1 T. cornstarch
1 t. vanilla extract

Heat milk and butter in a saucepan until almost boiling. Whisk in remaining ingredients.

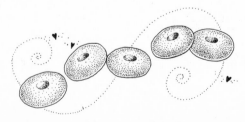

Doughnuts will be firmer if you allow them to stand
for 20 minutes before deep-frying.

KICK-OFF *Brunches*

Busy-Morning Breakfast Pizza

LaShelle Brown
Mulvane, KS

There's never a wrong time to eat pizza! This version is perfect for those mornings when you have friends over to watch the game.

2 8-oz. tubes refrigerated
    crescent rolls
1 lb. ground pork breakfast
    sausage, browned and
    drained

1 c. shredded Cheddar cheese
1 c. frozen shredded
    hashbrowns, thawed
5 eggs
1/4 c. milk

Unroll dough onto a 15"x10" jelly-roll pan, pressing seams together to seal. Evenly sprinkle sausage, hashbrowns and cheese over dough. In a bowl, beat together eggs and milk. Pour egg mixture over toppings on crust. Bake at 375 degrees for 30 to 35 minutes, until crust is browned and center of pizza is done. Serves 8 to 10.

Salami & Egg Sandwiches

Bonnie Zarch
Skokie, IL

These sandwiches may sound odd, but believe me, my two sons and husband devour them. Leftovers are good either reheated or cold from the fridge.

l lb. deli salami, chopped
12-oz. pkg. frozen diced onion,
    thawed
1 doz. eggs, beaten

8-oz. pkg. cream cheese,
    softened
8 kaiser rolls, split

In a large skillet over medium heat, brown salami and onion. Drain on paper towels; set aside. Scramble eggs in same skillet until they reach desired consistency; fold in salami mixture. Spread cream cheese evenly onto tops of rolls. Spoon egg mixture evenly onto bottoms of rolls; replace tops to make sandwiches. Makes 8 sandwiches.

Blueberry Pancake Cake

Dianne Cook
New Milford, CT

This delectable breakfast can be whipped up in a flash. Blueberry pancakes and sausage all in one? Doesn't get much better than that!

2 c. biscuit baking mix
1-1/4 c. milk
2 eggs
2 T. oil

1 pt. fresh blueberries
8-oz. pkg. brown & serve
  breakfast sausages, sliced

In a bowl, combine baking mix, milk, eggs and oil. Beat with an electric mixer on medium speed until smooth. Pour batter into a greased 13"x9" baking pan. Arrange berries and sausages on top. Bake at 350 degrees for 25 to 30 minutes. Serves 6 to 8.

Muffin-Tin Breakfast Quiche

Carla Belisle
Centuria, WI

These mini quiches are super for when company's coming over. Just pop a tin in the oven, and brunch is served in no time!

17.3-oz. pkg. frozen puff pastry,
  thawed
1 c. cooked ham, diced
1/2 c. red pepper, diced
1/2 c. sliced mushrooms
1/2 c. onion, minced

6 eggs, beaten
1 c. finely shredded Gouda
  cheese
0.9-oz. pkg. hollandaise sauce
  mix

Cut one sheet puff pastry into six 4-inch squares, reserving remaining sheet for another recipe. Press each square into a lightly greased deep muffin cup; set aside. In a bowl, combine ham, pepper, mushrooms and onion. To each muffin cup, add 1/2 cup beaten egg and one to 2 tablespoons of ham mixture. Top each cup evenly with cheese. Bake at 375 degrees for 20 minutes, or until pastry is golden and a toothpick inserted into the center tests clean. Meanwhile, prepare hollandaise sauce according to package directions. Drizzle each quiche with sauce before serving. Makes 6 servings.

KICK-OFF *Brunches*

Mother's Crispy Crumb Eggs

Tara Johnson
Logan, UT

This is a favorite recipe that my mother has cooked for us since we were young. Mom got up every morning and made sure we had a hot breakfast on the table. And now that I'm a mother, I do the same for my children.

2 T. butter
1-1/2 c. soft bread crumbs
8 eggs, beaten

10 slices bacon, crisply cooked
and crumbled

Melt butter in a large skillet over medium heat. Add bread crumbs to skillet and cook until golden. Remove bread crumbs from pan and set aside. Scramble eggs in the same skillet until they reach desired doneness. Sprinkle bacon and bread crumbs over eggs before serving. Serves 4.

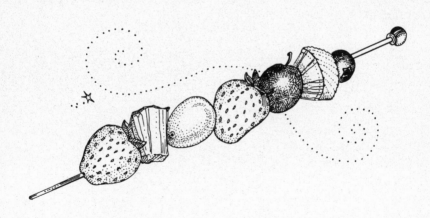

A fresh brunch side dish...fruit kabobs! Just slide pineapple chunks, apple slices, grapes, orange wedges and strawberries onto a wooden skewer. Easy to make, and no plate required!

Savory Sausage Squares

Bobbi Greene
Mount Juliet, TN

This dish is perfect for any get-together. It has only a few ingredients, it's easy to make and oh-so delicious! Be prepared to give out the recipe when you make it.

1 lb. spicy ground pork breakfast sausage
1/2 c. water
2 8-oz. tubes refrigerated seamless crescent roll dough, divided

8-oz. pkg. shredded Cheddar cheese
1 egg, beaten

Combine sausage and water in a skillet over medium heat. Cook and crumble until sausage is no longer pink; drain and set aside. Unroll one tube of crescent roll dough and place into a greased 13"x9" baking pan. Top dough with sausage; sprinkle with cheese. Unroll remaining tube of dough and place over cheese. Brush the top with egg. Bake, uncovered, at 350 degrees for 20 to 25 minutes, until golden. Cut into squares to serve. Serves 8 to 10.

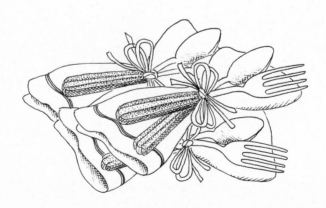

For a lunch or dinner-time treat, turn these Sausage Squares into Pizza Squares! Swap out the sausage for pepperoni and the Cheddar cheese for mozzarella. Add a little pizza sauce... so yummy!

KICK-OFF *Brunches*

Maple Monkey Bread

Susie Backus
Gooseberry Patch

This luscious, gooey monkey bread recipe is so easy to make and is perfect for special occasions! My ten-year-old daughter loves to help make this. A pizza cutter works great for cutting the dough.

1 c. brown sugar, packed
1-1/2 t. cinnamon
1/2 t. nutmeg
2 7-1/2 oz. tubes refrigerated
    buttermilk biscuits

1/2 c. butter, melted
1/2 c. chopped pecans
1/2 c. maple syrup

In a bowl, combine brown sugar, cinnamon and nutmeg; mix well. Separate biscuits and cut each biscuit into quarters. Dip each biscuit quarter into butter, then dredge in brown sugar mixture. Layer half of the coated biscuits in a greased Bundt® pan. Sprinkle with half the pecans. Arrange remaining biscuits over pecans; sprinkle with remaining pecans and any remaining brown sugar mixture. Drizzle maple syrup over all. Bake at 350 degrees for 25 to 35 minutes, until golden. Invert onto a plate and let stand 10 minutes before serving. Makes 6 to 8 servings.

Serve hot spiced coffee with your favorite game-day brunch dishes. Simply add 3/4 teaspoon apple pie spice to 1/2 cup ground coffee and brew as usual.

Sunday Bacon & Cheese Pull-Apart

Marcella Smith
Magnolia, OH

*We have this amazing dish every Sunday morning! I just
mix it up and pop it in the oven to bake while the kids and I
go about our morning routine...so easy!*

1 egg
2 T. milk
8-oz. tube refrigerated crescent
  rolls
5 slices bacon, crisply cooked
  and crumbled

1/2 c. pasteurized process cheese
  spread, cubed
1 t. garlic, minced
salt and pepper to taste

In a large bowl, beat together egg and milk. Cut each crescent roll
triangle into 4 pieces, rolling each piece into a ball. Add dough balls to
egg mixture and coat well. Fold in bacon, cheese and garlic. Spoon
mixture into a lightly greased 8"x8" baking pan, arranging pieces in a
single layer. Bake, uncovered, at 350 degrees for 30 to 35 minutes,
until golden. Serve warm. Serves 4.

Score big with football-shaped invitations cut from cardboard.
Jot the party information on the back, then for the football lacing,
tie on a white shoelace slipped through holes made with
a hole punch. Fun!

Gretta's Ham, Potato & Cheddar Quiche

Gretta DeMennato
Bel Air, MD

My family loves this delicious quiche. My two-year-old daughter gobbles it up and my four-year-old actually requests it! It's so easy to make...it allows me time to both play a game with my children and feed them well all on a busy weeknight.

9-inch pie crust
1 c. potato, boiled, peeled and
    diced
1 c. cooked ham, diced
2 t. oil
4 eggs, beaten

1/2 c. half-and-half
1 t. garlic powder
1 t. onion powder
salt and pepper to taste
1-1/4 c. shredded Cheddar
    cheese

Pierce sides and bottom of pie crust with a fork. Bake crust at 400 degrees for 5 minutes. Remove from oven and set aside. In a large skillet over medium-high heat, cook potato and ham in oil for 5 to 10 minutes, until golden. Remove from heat and let cool. Transfer potato mixture to pie crust. In a bowl, whisk together eggs, half-and-half and seasonings. Pour egg mixture over potato mixture in crust. Sprinkle with cheese. Bake, uncovered, at 350 degrees for 45 to 50 minutes. If edges of crust brown too quickly, cover with strips of aluminum foil. Cut into wedges. Serves 8.

If you're baking a quiche or brunch casserole at home before taking it to a potluck, keep it piping-hot by wrapping the baking pan in a layer of aluminum foil, then top with layers of newspaper.

Yummy Blueberry Coffee Cake

Karen Wald
Dalton, OH

I have been making this mouthwatering coffee cake for years! It's easy to make for pop-up brunches or gatherings. It comes together in a flash, and everyone loves the taste of the blueberries.

1-1/2 c. sugar, divided
1/4 c. canola oil
1 egg, beaten
1/2 c. buttermilk
1 c. whole-wheat flour
1-1/3 c. all-purpose flour,
   divided

2 t. baking powder
1/2 t. salt
2 c. fresh or frozen blueberries
2 T. butter, softened
1/2 t. cinnamon

In a bowl, beat together one cup sugar, oil and egg. Stir in buttermilk. Mix in whole-wheat flour, one cup all-purpose flour, baking powder and salt until well combined. Fold in blueberries. Spoon batter into a greased 11"x7" baking pan. In a separate bowl, combine butter, cinnamon, remaining sugar and remaining flour; mix until crumbs form. Sprinkle butter mixture over batter. Bake at 375 degrees for 35 to 40 minutes, until golden. Serves 8 to 10.

Add a splash of color to breakfast and brunch juices! Freeze strawberry slices or blueberries in ice cube trays. Toss several cubes into glasses of juice right before serving.

KICK-OFF *Brunches*

Sugared Bacon

Angie Venable
Gooseberry Patch

This bacon is soooo good! My family just can't get enough of it.

1-1/4 c. brown sugar, packed   1 lb. bacon, halved
1 T. cinnamon

In a bowl, combine brown sugar and cinnamon. Thoroughly coat each bacon half-slice with brown sugar mixture. Twist bacon slices and arrange on a lightly greased 15"x10" jelly-roll pan. Bake at 350 degrees for 15 to 20 minutes, until bacon is crisp and sugar is bubbly. Remove to sheets of aluminum foil to cool completely. Makes 16 servings.

Canadian Bacon Waffles

Jan Fishback
Carmi, IL

These are great, hearty waffles to whip up before heading out to tailgate for the big game...all the tasty flavors of a traditional breakfast packed into a waffle!

2 c. biscuit baking mix   1/2 c. Canadian bacon, chopped
2 eggs, lightly beaten   1/2 c. shredded Cheddar cheese
1/2 c. oil   Optional: 1 t. fresh chives,
1 c. club soda   snipped

In a bowl, combine baking mix, eggs and oil. Slowly add club soda; stir until smooth. Fold in Canadian bacon, cheese and chives, if using. Add batter by 1/2 cupfuls to a lightly greased waffle iron. Cook according to manufacturer's instructions. Makes about one dozen.

No-Bake Fruit & Nut Cereal Bars

Cheryl DeLorenzo
Paulsboro, NJ

Breakfast is important, but many of us are rushed in the morning. So I keep these bars on hand because they're perfect to grab and go, providing a tasty and healthy homemade breakfast treat.

4 c. multi-grain oats and honey
  cereal
1/2 c. salted peanuts
1/2 c. sweetened flaked coconut
1/2 c. dried apricots, chopped
1/2 c. raisins

1/2 c. dried cranberries
3/4 c. brown sugar, packed
1/2 c. corn syrup
1/4 c. creamy peanut butter
1 t. vanilla extract

In a large bowl, combine cereal, peanuts, coconut and fruit. Mix well and set aside. In a saucepan over medium heat, combine remaining ingredients except vanilla. Cook, stirring constantly, until mixture comes to a boil. Boil for one minute; remove from heat and stir in vanilla. Drizzle hot syrup over cereal mixture. Mix well with a greased spoon; press firmly into a lightly greased 13"x9" baking pan. Let stand until cool. Cut into bars. Store in an airtight container. Makes about one dozen.

A charming gift for anyone! Arrange No-Bake Fruit & Nut Cereal Bars on a mini cutting board. Wrap clear plastic wrap around them to keep extra fresh, and tie a big checkered ribbon around the handle.

Good Morning Biscuits & Gravy

Naomi Townsend
Ozark, MO

This is a combination of my mother's biscuit recipe and my sausage gravy recipe. It's a family favorite for breakfast, but we often eat it for other meals too. The sausage gravy is also delightful served over hashbrowns!

2-1/2 c. all-purpose flour,
   divided
1 T. baking powder
1 t. salt
1/4 c. shortening

4-3/4 c. milk, divided
1 lb. ground pork breakfast
   sausage
salt and pepper to taste

In a bowl, combine 2 cups flour, baking powder and salt. Cut in shortening until small crumbs form. Add 3/4 cup milk; stir until just moistened. Transfer dough to a lightly floured surface. Knead dough 5 to 10 times; roll out to 1/2-inch thickness. Cut with a floured biscuit cutter. Transfer biscuits to an ungreased baking sheet. Bake at 450 degrees for 10 to 12 minutes, until golden. Meanwhile, brown and crumble sausage in a skillet over medium heat. Stir in remaining flour. Gradually pour in remaining milk and cook until gravy reaches desired consistency. Season with salt and pepper. To serve, split biscuits and top with sausage gravy. Serves 6.

A fragrant morning surprise for brunch guests! Gather some fresh blooms in your favorite team's colors and place in a big glass vase for a brunch centerpiece. So sweet!

Pumpkin-Caramel Doughnut Holes

Amy Bradsher
Roxboro, NC

One day, my daughter and I experimented with some pumpkin and came up with these yummy doughnut holes. We love the gooey sweetness of the caramel glaze on top...my husband says that they're perfect fresh from the oven!

2 c. white whole-wheat flour
2 t. cinnamon
1-1/2 t. baking powder
1-1/2 t. baking soda
1/2 t. salt
1/4 c. butter, softened

1/3 c. brown sugar, packed
1 egg, beaten
15-oz. can pumpkin
1/3 to 1/2 c. milk
3/4 c. sour cream
Optional: 1/2 c. chocolate chips

In a bowl, mix together flour, cinnamon, baking powder, baking soda and salt; set aside. In a separate large bowl, beat together butter and brown sugar. Mix in egg, pumpkin, milk and sour cream. Slowly mix flour mixture into egg mixture until just combined; add chocolate chips, if using. Batter will be thick. Lightly grease a mini muffin tin. Add a tablespoon of batter to each mini muffin cup. Bake at 325 degrees for 10 to 15 minutes, until a toothpick tests clean. Cool in pan for 2 to 3 minutes. Remove from pan and cool completely. Dip doughnut holes into Caramel Glaze before serving. Serves 6.

Caramel Glaze:

1 c. powdered sugar
1 to 2 T. caramel ice cream
    topping

2 T. milk

In a bowl, stir together all ingredients.

Major League
Munchies

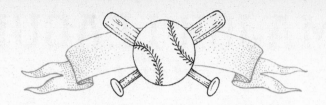

Deluxe Texas Nachos

Angy Cooper
Olathe, KS

*I love nachos, but not the way most restaurants make them.
So I created my own super-duper recipe...perfect for
game-day snacking!*

1 lb. ground beef
1 T. chili powder
4-oz. can chopped green chiles
14-1/2 oz. can diced tomatoes,
   drained
15-1/2 oz. can chili beans

32-oz. pkg. bite-size tortilla
   chips
12-oz. pkg. shredded
   Mexican-blend cheese
Garnish: sour cream, guacamole,
   chunky salsa

Brown beef in a skillet over medium heat; drain. When almost cooked through, stir in chili powder and green chiles. Continue cooking until beef is no longer pink; stir in tomatoes and beans. Reduce heat and simmer for 3 to 4 minutes, until thickened. Meanwhile, evenly divide chips among 5 to 6 serving bowls. Spoon beef mixture over chips. Sprinkle servings with desired amount of cheese; garnish as desired. Serves 5 to 6.

If you love super-spicy foods, give New Mexico chili powder a try. Sold at Hispanic and specialty food stores, it contains pure ground red chili peppers, unlike regular chili powder which is a blend of chili, garlic and other seasonings.

MAJOR LEAGUE
Munchies

Slow-Cooker Buffalo Chicken Nachos
Rachel Hodges
Omaha, AR

These yummy nachos are a savory, spicy treat. It's a breeze to make them in the slow cooker. Plus, you can make the recipe even easier by using chicken tenderloins instead of breasts...just cut the cooking time in half!

1 lb. boneless, skinless chicken breasts
garlic salt to taste
salt and pepper to taste
12-oz. bottle buffalo wing sauce
1/2 c. ranch salad dressing
1/2 lb. pasteurized process cheese spread, cubed
10-oz. can diced tomatoes with green chiles
12-oz. pkg. tortilla chips

Place chicken in a slow cooker; sprinkle with garlic salt, salt and pepper. Pour in enough buffalo wing sauce to cover chicken. Cover and cook on low setting until very tender, about 4 hours. Shred chicken with 2 forks and drain off any excess liquid. Stir in salad dressing. In a saucepan, combine cheese and tomatoes with green chiles. Cook and stir until cheese melts. Layer tortilla chips on a large serving plate. Spoon cheese sauce over chips; top with chicken. Serves 6 to 8.

To shred cooked chicken, use two forks and insert the prongs, back sides facing each other, into the center of a portion of meat. Then simply pull the forks gently away from each other.

Easy Cheesy Bean Dip

Carmen Hyde
Spencerville, IN

This bean dip is requested at almost every gathering! A lot of times when we go camping, I'll take my slow cooker and all the ingredients with us. Then I just whip it up in the slow cooker, and this tasty dip is ready by lunchtime!

1/2 lb. ground beef
8-oz. pkg. cream cheese,
　softened
16-oz. can refried beans
1 c. sour cream
1-1/2 t. onion powder

2 T. taco seasoning mix
8-oz. pkg. shredded Colby Jack
　cheese
Garnish: chopped tomato, sliced
　black olives, guacamole
tortilla chips

Brown beef in a skillet over medium heat; drain. In a large bowl, combine beef with remaining ingredients except shredded cheese, garnish and chips. Layer half the beef mixture in a slow cooker; top with half the shredded cheese. Repeat layers. Cover and cook on low setting for 3 to 4 hours. Garnish as desired; serve with chips. Serves 12.

Get creative at your next game-day get-together and serve your dips in unexpected serving "dishes" such as hollowed-out vegetables, breads or even beer mugs.

Black Bean Salsa

Teresa Eller
Tonganoxie, KS

This is a perfect dip to make for guests. Just mix it up the night before and pop it in the fridge. When everyone arrives the next day, all you have to do is set it on the table...how easy is that?

12-oz. pkg. frozen corn
15-oz. can black beans, drained
    and rinsed
14-1/2 oz. can diced tomatoes,
    drained
1 green onion, chopped
1 green pepper, chopped
1/2 t. chili powder
1 t. salt
tortilla chips

Cook corn according to package directions; cool. In a bowl, combine corn and remaining ingredients except tortilla chips; mix well. Cover and refrigerate overnight. Serve with chips for dipping. Serves 6.

Make your own baked tortilla chips...it's easy. Spritz both sides of corn or flour tortillas with non-stick vegetable spray. Cut into wedges and microwave on high setting for 5 to 6 minutes, turning wedges over every 1-1/2 minutes. Sprinkle warm chips with sea salt and serve.

Party Cocktail Sausages

LaDeana Cooper
Batavia, OH

This is an easy slow-cooker treat for any special occasion. Set these on your buffet table and just watch them disappear! I like to add some cayenne pepper, red pepper flakes or chopped jalapeños for a little added kick.

12-oz. jar chili sauce
8-oz. jar grape jelly
Optional: 1 to 2 seeded and
    chopped jalapeños or
    1/2 t. red pepper flakes

14-oz. pkg. mini smoked
    sausages

Whisk together chili sauce, jelly and jalapeño or red pepper flakes, if using, in a slow cooker. Fold in sausages; mix well. Cover and cook on low setting for 4 hours. Serves 8 to 10.

Chase & Brady's Bacon Puffs

Stacy Lamontagne
Kennebunk, ME

My sister-in-law made these once for a football game. They've become a family favorite in my house, and my son asks for them every time we watch the New England Patriots. Go Pats!

1 lb. bacon

32-oz. pkg. frozen potato puffs

Cut bacon slices crosswise into thirds. Wrap each potato puff with a piece of bacon; arrange on an ungreased baking sheet, seam-side down. Bake at 450 degrees for 20 to 25 minutes, until potato puffs are golden and bacon is crisp. Serves 10 to 12.

MAJOR LEAGUE
Munchies

Amanda's Spicy Sweet Potato Fries

Amanda Carew
Mount Pearl, NL

These fries go with just about everything! We serve them with sour cream on the side for dipping...so tasty! Sometimes I'll sprinkle the cayenne pepper into the sour cream instead of on the fries so those who don't like spicy foods can enjoy these fries too.

1-1/2 t. pepper
1-1/2 t. onion powder
1-1/2 t. garlic powder
1/4 t. salt
1/8 t. cayenne pepper

4 to 6 sweet potatoes, sliced
  into thin wedges
1/4 c. olive oil
Garnish: sour cream

In a small bowl, combine seasonings; set aside. Place potato wedges in a separate bowl and drizzle with olive oil; toss to coat evenly. Sprinkle seasoning mixture over potatoes; toss. Transfer potatoes to a lightly greased baking sheet. Bake at 350 degrees for 25 to 30 minutes, turning potatoes every 10 minutes, until crisp and tender. Serve with sour cream for dipping. Makes 4 to 6 servings.

Have appetizers for dinner! Set up a family-size sampler
with Amanda's Spicy Sweet Potato Fries, mini pizza snacks,
mini egg rolls, potato skins and a bunch of dippers to try too.
Don't forget the French fries!

Fried Dill Pickles

Karen McCann
Marion, OH

*Fried pickles may sound strange, but they're incredibly yummy.
One bite and you'll be hooked! The horseradish dipping sauce takes
these tasty treats to a whole new level of scrumptious.*

3 c. sliced dill pickles, well
    drained
2 c. all-purpose flour
1/2 t. salt

1/4 t. pepper
2 eggs
1 c. milk
oil for deep frying

Pat pickles with paper towels; set aside. Combine flour, salt and pepper
in a small bowl. In a separate bowl, beat together eggs and milk. Pour
2 inches of oil into a large saucepan; heat to 375 degrees. Working in
batches, dip pickle slices into egg mixture, then dredge with flour
mixture. Fry in oil until golden, about 8 to 10 minutes, carefully turning
once. Transfer to paper towels to drain. Serve with Horseradish Sauce
for dipping. Serves 4.

Horseradish Sauce:

1/2 c. prepared horseradish
1/4 c. mayonnaise
1 t. whole-grain mustard

1/3 c. beer or non-alcoholic beer
1/2 t. sugar
1/2 t. salt

In a bowl, mix together all ingredients. Cover and refrigerate for at least
one hour before serving.

Whole-grain mustard is so rich and
flavorful. The mustard seeds haven't
been ground, giving it a coarse texture.

MAJOR LEAGUE
Munchies

Loaded Deviled Eggs

Kim McCallie
Guyton, GA

*I created this recipe to combine two of my husband's favorite dishes...
chicken salad and deviled eggs. The two flavors come together
so well, and they're perfect for picnics and tailgating.*

1 doz. eggs, hard-boiled, peeled
   and halved
1-1/2 lbs. chicken, cooked and
   shredded
3 green onions, finely chopped
1 c. mayonnaise
1 T. yellow mustard

1 T. Dijon mustard
1/4 t. coarse pepper
1/4 t. celery seed
1/4 t. garlic salt
1/4 t. paprika
Optional: additional paprika

Transfer egg yolks to a bowl and mash; set egg whites aside. Add
chicken and green onions to egg yolks; mix well. In a separate small
bowl, mix together mayonnaise, mustards and seasonings. Spoon
mayonnaise mixture into chicken mixture and stir well to combine. Fill
each egg white half with a tablespoon of filling. Sprinkle with paprika
before serving, if desired. Makes 2 dozen.

Toting deviled eggs to a carry-in? Nestle the eggs in a bed of
shredded lettuce or curly parsley to keep them from
sliding around...they'll arrive looking scrumptious!

Herbed Deviled Eggs

JoAnn

Deviled eggs are a tasty dish to take to parties. These take the classic taste of deviled eggs and spruce it up a bit with some flavorful fresh herbs and a little spice!

1 doz. eggs, hard-boiled, peeled
  and halved
2 T. fresh chives, minced
2 T. fresh parsley, minced
1/4 c. sour cream

1 T. lemon juice
1/2 t. curry powder
salt, pepper and cayenne pepper
  to taste

Transfer egg yolks to a bowl and mash; set egg whites aside. Add remaining ingredients to egg yolks; mix well. Fill each egg white half with a tablespoon of filling. Chill at least one hour before serving. Makes one dozen.

Making deviled eggs? Whip 'em up in no time by combining filling ingredients in a plastic zipping bag instead of a bowl. Blend by squeezing the bag, snip off a corner and pipe the filling into the whites...what could be easier?

MAJOR LEAGUE
Munchies

Uncle Bruce's Snack Mix

Laura Anderson
Indianola, IA

I have fond memories of making this mix with my Uncle Bruce when I was little. It is still a favorite snack to this day, and it always makes an appearance at family gatherings. It's hard to stop munching on this mix!

3 c. baked cheese snack crackers
3 c. oyster crackers
1/4 c. oil
0.4-oz. pkg. buttermilk ranch
   salad dressing mix
1-1/2 t. dill weed

Combine all ingredients in a brown paper bag. Close bag and shake well, coating crackers evenly with seasonings and oil. Keep bag closed. Let stand overnight before serving. Makes 6 cups.

Touchdown Toss

Dori Cron
Paradise, CA

We are football fanatics! So on game night, everything has to be ready before kickoff. This is a good make-ahead recipe for tight schedules. It is simple, delicious and sure to please.

3 c. doughnut-shaped oat cereal
3 c. bite-size crispy corn cereal
   squares
3 c. cookie-shaped cereal
3 c. pretzel sticks, broken
3 c. graham crackers, broken
1 c. sunflower kernels
2 c. candy-coated chocolates
3 c. salted roasted mixed nuts
3 lbs. white melting chocolate,
   chopped

In a large bowl, combine all ingredients except white chocolate. Place chocolate in a microwave-safe bowl. Microwave on high for one minute; stir well. Continue to microwave at 30-second intervals until chocolate is completely melted. Pour melted chocolate over cereal mixture; stir to coat well. Transfer cereal mixture to 2 ungreased 15"x10" jelly-roll pans. Spread cereal mixture evenly on pans; refrigerate for about 45 minutes, or until chocolate is set. Break into pieces. Makes about 24 cups.

Cajun Boiled Peanuts

Michelle Marberry
Valley, AL

A tailgating staple in the South! Leave out the crab boil and hot sauce if you prefer them plain. These may take a little time to make in the slow cooker, but they're definitely worth it!

2 lbs. raw peanuts in shells
1 c. salt
3-oz. pkg. crab boil seasoning
  mix

1/2 c. hot pepper sauce
12 c. water

Combine all ingredients in a 6-quart slow cooker. Cover and cook on high setting for 18 hours, or until peanuts are soft. Drain and serve. Makes about 2 pounds.

Sweet Chipotle Pretzels

Geraldine Saucier
Albuquerque, NM

This is a quick and tasty snack to make for any occasion. It's especially great for watching movies, playing games, study group munchies or whenever you need a sweet snack!

1 egg white
1 t. water
2-1/2 c. mini pretzel twists
1/2 c. brown sugar, packed

1-1/2 t. cinnamon
1/4 t. allspice
1/8 t. chipotle chili powder

In a small bowl, whisk together egg white and water until frothy. Place pretzels in a separate large bowl. Pour egg white mixture over pretzels; toss until well coated. Drain off any excess egg white and set pretzels aside. In a large plastic zipping bag, combine remaining ingredients. Close bag and shake well to combine seasonings. Add pretzels to bag. Close bag and shake well to coat evenly. Arrange coated pretzels in a single layer on a parchment paper-lined baking sheet. Bake pretzels at 350 degrees for 10 minutes, turning pretzels halfway through. Cool completely. Store in an airtight container. Makes about 2-1/2 cups.

Slow-Cooker Spinach & Artichoke Dip

Angie Ellefson
Milton, WI

This is the best spinach & artichoke dip I've ever tasted...my family & friends agree! It's always requested for get-togethers. Any leftovers make a perfect spread for grilled chicken sandwiches.

10-oz. pkg. frozen chopped spinach, thawed and drained
13-oz. can artichoke hearts, drained and chopped
7-oz. pkg. shredded mozzarella and Asiago cheese blend with roasted garlic
6-oz. pkg. shredded Asiago and Parmesan cheese blend
8-oz. pkg low-fat cream cheese, cubed
1 c. light sour cream
1 c. light mayonnaise
3 T. garlic, minced
white pepper to taste
1/4 to 1/3 c. milk
assorted dippers, such as toasted baguette slices and corn chips

Combine all ingredients except milk and dippers in a slow cooker. Cover and cook on high setting for 2 hours, or until cheese is melted. Stir in milk until desired dipping consistency is reached. Turn slow cooker to low setting. Serve with assorted dippers. Makes 8 to 10 servings.

Shape a deflated new basketball, football or soccer ball into a bowl and fill it to the rim with corn chips or extra baguette slices for Slow-Cooker Spinach & Artichoke Dip!

Charlie's Steakhouse Cheese Spread
Barb Henderson
Everton, AR

Charlie's Steakhouse was a beloved restaurant in Massachusetts, but is now long out of business. They always served this dip to folks while they waited for their meals to be served. Somehow my mother got the recipe from them back in the '40s, and it has since been an absolute family favorite!

8-oz. pkg. cream cheese, softened
2 T. onion, minced
1-1/2 t. catsup
1-1/2 t. sour cream
2 T. sweet pickle relish
salt and pepper to taste

3 green olives with pimentos, diced
1 clove garlic, minced
1/2 t. dry mustard
1/2 t. Worcestershire sauce
assorted dippers such as celery, carrots and green onions

Combine all ingredients except dippers in a large bowl; mix well. Cover and refrigerate for 2 hours to overnight. Serve with dippers. Serves 8 to 10.

To remove the smell of garlic from your hands, simply rub your hands with a stainless steel spoon or other utensil while holding them under cold running water.

MAJOR LEAGUE
Munchies

Mixed-Up Olive Dip

Lori Haines
Johnson City, TN

My family and I absolutely love olives! Pitted ones, unpitted ones, black, green, stuffed, unstuffed...you name it. My siblings and I are always looking for a new olive dish to introduce. I found this olive dip recipe recently and it turned out wonderfully. I hope that your olive-loving gang will love it as much as mine does.

5-1/4 oz. jar green olives with
   pimentos, drained
6-oz. can black olives, drained
2 stalks celery, sliced into 2-inch
   pieces
1 t. onion powder

1 t. Italian seasoning
2 t. garlic, minced
1/4 c. extra-virgin olive oil
assorted dippers such as French
   bread slices, Melba toast,
   crackers and raw veggies

Combine all ingredients except oil and dippers in a food processor. Pulse until olives and celery are finely minced. Stir in oil. Transfer to a serving bowl. Cover and refrigerate for 4 hours to overnight. Serve with assorted dippers. Also can be used as a sandwich spread or tapenade. Serves 10.

Olive trees are very hardy and can live to be a great age.
There are some olive trees, still living and producing olives,
that are over 1,500 years old!

Creamy Crabby Dip

Wendy Lee Paffenroth
Pine Island, NY

My guys love this dip as a snack at halftime during college football games. You can make it hotter by adding more horseradish or hot pepper sauce if you like.

8-oz. pkg. cream cheese,
  softened
6-oz. can crabmeat, drained
2 t. onion, grated
1 T. milk
salt and pepper to taste
1 T. prepared horseradish

1 T. hot pepper sauce
1/4 c. roasted red pepper, diced
Garnish: chopped fresh parsley,
  paprika
assorted dippers such as
  crackers, fresh veggies and
  Melba toast

In a lightly greased 2-quart casserole dish, combine all ingredients except garnish and dippers; stir to mix well. Bake, uncovered, at 325 degrees for 10 minutes, or until bubbly. Sprinkle with parsley and paprika. Serve with assorted dippers. Serves 4 to 6.

Crab & Shrimp Poppers

Gladys Brehm
Quakertown, PA

This recipe tastes amazing with either crab or shrimp! Or, if you're feeling adventurous, why not try a little bit of each?

8-oz. pkg. cream cheese softened
6-oz. can crabmeat or tiny
  shrimp, drained
1 onion, minced

12-oz. pkg. frozen wonton
  wrappers, thawed
oil for deep frying
Garnish: sour cream

In a bowl, combine cream cheese and crab or shrimp; mix well. Stir in onion. Spoon one teaspoon cream cheese mixture into each wonton wrapper. Fold sides of wrapper over filling; pinch to seal. Pour several inches of oil into a deep saucepan over medium-high heat; heat to 370 degrees. Fry wontons, a few at a time, in hot oil until golden. Drain on paper towels. Serve with sour cream for dipping. Serves 6.

MAJOR LEAGUE
Munchies

Spicy BBQ Chicken Wings

Julie Saifullah
Lexington, KY

I first discovered this simple recipe when we had a hungry teenage boy in the house. After a few modifications, we now have a family favorite! These wings are easy to make, bake and take.

2-1/2 lbs. chicken wings
1 c. barbecue sauce

1/4 c. hot pepper sauce

Place wings in a lightly greased 13"x9" baking pan. Bake at 400 degrees for 20 minutes. Remove wings from oven; drain. Flip wings and bake for another 20 minutes. Meanwhile, combine barbecue sauce and hot pepper sauce in a bowl. Add sauce to wings in pan; stir until evenly coated. Bake for another 30 minutes, or until wings are cooked through and sauce is thickened. Serves 6 to 8.

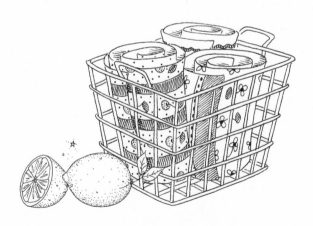

A tray of warm, moistened towels is a must when serving sticky barbecue ribs or chicken wings! Dampen fingertip towels in water and a dash of lemon juice, roll up and microwave on high for 10 to 15 seconds.

Hearty Slow-Cooker Nachos

Stacy Lane
Lewes, DE

I recently tried this recipe, and my family loves it! It's so easy to make, and it's really yummy. Great for football games or for a quick get-together.

2 T. oil
1 onion, chopped
1 green pepper, chopped
1 lb. ground beef
10-3/4 oz. can cream of
  mushroom soup
1-1/4 oz. low-sodium taco
  seasoning mix

8-oz. jar taco sauce
16-oz. can vegetarian refried
  beans
2 c. shredded Cheddar cheese
Garnish: shredded lettuce, sliced
  tomato, sour cream
tortilla chips

Heat oil in a large skillet over medium heat. Sauté onion and pepper in oil until softened. Add beef; cook until browned. Drain; spoon beef mixture into a slow cooker. Add remaining ingredients except garnish and chips; mix well. Cover and cook on high setting for one hour, or on low setting for 2 to 2-1/2 hours. Serve with chips. Garnish individual servings with lettuce, tomato and sour cream. Serves 8.

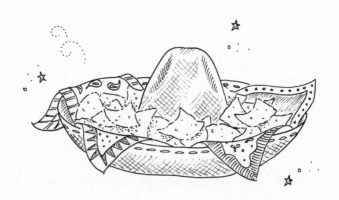

For a Mexican-inspired fiesta, dress up the table in south-of-the-border style...arrange colorful woven blankets, sombreros and tissue paper flowers around the room!

MAJOR LEAGUE
Munchies

Pepperoni Bread

Charlotte Smith
Tyrone, PA

Pepperoni bread is just one of those treats everyone loves...big and small, young and old. Try serving slices of this bread with some warmed pizza sauce for dipping. You never have to worry about leftovers, because there won't be any!

1 loaf frozen bread dough,
   thawed
1 egg, beaten
1/2 t. dried parsley
1/4 t. dried oregano
1/4 t. garlic salt

1/4 to 1/2 c. grated Parmesan
   cheese
1/4 to 1/2 lb. pepperoni, sliced
1/4 to 1/2 lb. provolone cheese,
   sliced

Let dough rise according to package directions. Meanwhile, combine egg, seasonings and Parmesan cheese in a bowl. Divide dough into 2 equal pieces. Roll out one piece of dough into a 10-inch by 8-inch rectangle, about 1/2-inch thick; spread with half of egg mixture. Evenly arrange half the pepperoni and half the provolone cheese over top. Roll up, starting at a long side, pinching seams together to seal. Repeat process for remaining ingredients. Transfer loaves to an ungreased baking sheet, seam-side down. Bake at 350 degrees for 35 minutes, or until golden. Slice to serve. Serves 8.

Why not use pizza dough to make Pepperoni Bread?
Your favorite local pizza shop may be more than happy
to sell you a ball of their tasty dough for you to use at home!

Pizza Muffins

Vickie

*These scrumptious little treats are perfect for serving a crowd.
They come together in a flash, and your guests will
definitely be back for more.*

6 English muffins, split
3/4 c. pizza sauce
3-1/2 oz. pkg. sliced pepperoni
1/2 lb. ground pork sausage,
    browned and drained

8-oz. pkg. sliced mushrooms
1/2 onion, chopped
8-oz. pkg. shredded mozzarella
    cheese

Toast English muffin halves. Spoon sauce evenly over each half. Layer
with remaining ingredients in the order given. Place on an ungreased
baking sheet. Bake at 375 degrees for 5 to 10 minutes, until cheese is
golden and bubbly. Makes one dozen.

Turn Pizza Muffins into Pizza Bites! Just cut each muffin
into quarters for bite-size appetizers. Stick a toothpick
in each and watch them disappear.

MAJOR LEAGUE
Munchies

Healthy Jalapeño Poppers

Sarah Timpa-Funderburg
Westlake, LA

I was on a diet for a while, so I made some changes to one of my favorite appetizers, jalapeño poppers. I loved them so much that I brought them to one of our family gatherings. I didn't tell anyone that they were a "diet food," and everyone loved them.

1 T. olive oil
1/2 lb. ground turkey breast
3/4 c. green pepper, finely
    chopped
1/2 c. onion, finely chopped
1 clove garlic, minced
1/2 c. fat-free cream cheese,
    softened

Greek seasoning to taste
10 jalapeño peppers, halved and
    seeded
Garnish: low-fat Parmesan
    cheese

Heat oil in a skillet over medium heat. Brown turkey with green pepper, onion and garlic; drain. Transfer turkey mixture to a bowl; blend in cream cheese and seasoning. Add one tablespoon of turkey mixture to each jalapeño half; sprinkle with Parmesan cheese. Transfer filled jalapeños to lightly greased baking sheets. Bake at 425 degrees for 15 to 20 minutes, or until tops are golden. Makes 20 servings.

When making any dish with hot peppers as an ingredient, it's always a good idea to wear a pair of plastic gloves to protect your skin while slicing or chopping the peppers.

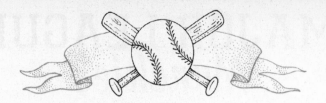

3-Cheese Beer Fondue

Sonya Labbe
Los Angeles, CA

*Each time I want to slow down, I serve a fondue. It encourages
everybody to take it slow and to enjoy the food and
each other's company.*

1/2 head cauliflower, cut into
flowerets
1/2 bunch broccoli, cut into
flowerets
1 c. shredded Cheddar cheese
1 c. shredded Gruyère cheese

1 c. shredded Swiss cheese
1 T. all-purpose flour
1-1/2 c. beer or non-alcoholic
beer
2 T. Dijon mustard
1 baguette loaf, cubed

Bring a large saucepan of water to a boil over medium-high heat. Add
cauliflower and broccoli to pot; cook for 2 minutes. Drain, rinse in cold
water and set aside. In a bowl, combine cheeses and flour; toss to mix
and set aside. Pour beer into a small saucepan and bring to a simmer
over medium heat. Reduce heat to low and add cheese mixture, a little
at a time, stirring constantly. After cheese is melted, add mustard.
Transfer cheese mixture to a warm fondue pot. Arrange cauliflower,
broccoli and baguette pieces around fondue pot for dipping. Serves 6.

Fondue pots do double duty for more than just fondue. They're
ideal for keeping dips or meatballs warm.

MAJOR LEAGUE
Munchies

Game-Day Piggies

Wendy Ball
Battle Creek, MI

I came up with this variation based on one of my other favorite recipes. Instead of pepperoni and mozzarella, I use hot dogs, Polish sausage or Kielbasa dogs.

12-oz. pkg. hot dogs
16 frozen dinner rolls, thawed
32-oz. jar sauerkraut, drained
1 c. shredded sharp Cheddar
   cheese
1 egg

1 t. water
Optional: poppy seed or sesame
   seed
Garnish: catsup, mustard,
   barbecue sauce

Cut each hot dog in half crosswise; set aside. Roll out each roll into a 5-inch circle. Place a hot dog piece on each circle; sprinkle each with some sauerkraut and cheese. Roll up dough, pinching together edges to seal. Arrange dough-wrapped hot dogs, seam-side down, on a lightly greased baking sheet; cover and let rise for 30 to 45 minutes. Meanwhile, whisk together egg and water in a small bowl. Brush each hot dog with egg mixture; sprinkle with poppy seed or sesame seed, if using. Bake at 350 degrees for 18 to 20 minutes, until golden. Let cool on baking sheet for 5 minutes. Serve with catsup, mustard or barbecue sauce for dipping. Serves 8 to 10.

A vintage muffin tin is perfect for serving a variety of savory dips and spreads. Just spoon a different flavor into each muffin cup.

Straight From Buffalo Chicken Wing Dip

Julie Stuart
Lockport, NY

I have lived right outside of Buffalo, New York my entire life, and have eaten more chicken wings than I can count. This dip is just terrific and is certainly a lot less messy than eating the real thing!

2 8-oz. pkgs. cream cheese, softened
1-1/2 lbs. boneless, skinless chicken breasts, cooked and cubed

12-oz. bottle hot pepper sauce
15-oz. jar blue cheese salad dressing

Spread cream cheese in an ungreased 13"x9" baking pan; set aside. In a bowl, combine chicken and hot pepper sauce; mix to coat well. Spread chicken mixture over cream cheese. Bake at 350 degrees for 30 minutes. Top with salad dressing. Serves 10 to 12.

When it comes to tailgating dippers, serve up lots of variety...
hearty crackers, pretzel rods, crisp veggies or slices of thick
sourdough or pumpernickel bread. All are just right
for creamy dips and spreads.

MAJOR LEAGUE
Munchies

Mexican Egg Rolls

Jamie Mills
Springfield, KY

This snack is one of my family's favorites! We like eating these while watching football.

1 T. oil
1/2 c. onion, finely chopped
2 boneless, skinless chicken breasts, cooked and shredded
4-oz. can chopped green chiles
1/2 c. chicken broth
1/2 t. garlic, minced

salt and pepper to taste
12 egg roll or wonton wrappers
1 to 2 c. shredded sharp Cheddar cheese
oil for deep frying
Garnish: guacamole, salsa, sour cream

Heat oil in a large skillet over medium heat. Sauté onion in oil until translucent. Add chicken, chiles, broth, garlic, salt and pepper. Simmer until mixture thickens and most of the liquid cooks out. Divide mixture evenly among egg roll or wonton wrappers; top each with some cheese. Roll up and pinch seams together. Heat several inches of oil to 375 degrees in a saucepan over medium-high heat. Fry rolls in oil, a few at a time, until golden on all sides. Drain on paper towels. Serve with guacamole, salsa and sour cream for dipping. Serves 4 to 6.

Turn up the heat! Try using extra-spicy salsa, Mexican-blend cheese or hot ground pork sausage in Mexican Egg Rolls for some extra zing.

Gridiron Guacamole

Danielle Gniadek
South Boston, MA

Guacamole is such an easy and mouthwatering dip. One day I was really craving it, so I decided to make my own. A little cumin, a little cilantro...before I knew it, I created my favorite guacamole!

2 avocados, halved, pitted and
    diced
juice of 1 lime
1 tomato, diced

1/2 red onion, chopped
2-1/2 T. fresh cilantro, chopped
1 T. ground cumin
salt and pepper to taste

Place diced avocados in a bowl; sprinkle with lime juice. Fold in onion, tomato and cilantro; sprinkle with seasonings. Using a fork or potato masher, mash and mix avocado mixture to desired consistency, leaving slightly lumpy. Serves 4.

Pico de Gallo

Susan Oliver
Riverside, CA

This is my family's favorite homemade pico de gallo recipe. We use the tomatoes and cilantro that we grow in our garden. It's the most popular dip on the table at family gatherings!

2 c. tomatoes, diced
1/2 c. onion, diced
2 T. fresh cilantro, chopped

2 t. freshly squeezed lime juice
1/2 t. salt
tortilla chips

Combine all ingredients in a bowl; mix well. Cover and let stand 30 minutes for flavors to blend. Serve with chips for dipping. Serves 4.

If a bunch of fresh herbs is starting to droop, just snip the stems and place the bunch in a glass of cold water; loosely cover leaves with a plastic bag, and chill. It will perk up in no time.

MAJOR LEAGUE
Munchies

Beer-Battered Fried Veggies

Rhonda Reeder
Ellicott City, MD

Sometimes I just get bored with the same ol' French fries, mozzarella sticks and fried mushrooms for appetizers. So I tried frying up some of my other favorite vegetables too. They turned out so tasty. The batter is nice and fluffy and the vegetables still have a wonderful crunch to them!

2 c. all-purpose flour, divided
1-1/2 c. beer or non-alcoholic
   beer
2 eggs, beaten
1 c. milk
salt and pepper to taste

oil for deep frying
1 carrot, peeled and sliced
1 onion, sliced and separated
   into rings
6 mushrooms, stems removed
1 green pepper, sliced

In a bowl, mix together 1-1/2 cups flour and beer; let stand 30 minutes. In a separate bowl, whisk together eggs and milk. In a shallow bowl, mix together remaining flour, salt and pepper. Heat several inches of oil to 375 degrees in a deep skillet over medium-high heat. Dip each vegetable slice into egg mixture, then into flour and seasoning mixture, finally into batter. Fry vegetables, a few at a time, in oil until golden, about 3 to 5 minutes. Drain on paper towels. Serves 6.

Save time on kitchen clean-up...always use a spatter screen when frying in a skillet or Dutch oven.

Grandma Hovey's Party Meatballs

Nicole Knoepke
Dahlonega, GA

These slow-cooker meatballs are perfect for get-togethers or tailgating. Just put all the ingredients in the slow cooker, turn it on and walk away...how easy is that? These scrumptious little treats will be ready before you know it.

5-lb. pkg. frozen meatballs, thawed
10-3/4 oz. can cream of mushroom soup
10-3/4 oz. can cream of chicken soup
16-oz. container sour cream
2 8-oz. pkgs. cream cheese, softened
1 T. dried, minced onion
1 T. dill weed
1 T. garlic powder

Place meatballs in a large slow cooker. In a bowl, mix together remaining ingredients; spoon over meatballs. Stir to combine. Cover and cook on low setting for 4 to 4-1/2 hours. Serves 15.

Use mini pretzel sticks instead of toothpicks to serve snacks like meatballs, mini smoked sausages and cheese cubes.

MAJOR LEAGUE
Munchies

Ragin' Cajun Mozzarella Sticks

Jill Ross
Pickerington, OH

If I was only able to eat one appetizer for the rest of my life, I would choose these delicious mozzarella sticks. All the gooey cheese and crisp, spicy batter...they're just too good to pass up! These are loads better than any mozzarella sticks you can get in restaurants.

2 eggs
1/4 c. water
1-1/2 c. Italian-flavored dry
    bread crumbs
1/2 t. Cajun seasoning
1/2 t. garlic salt

2/3 c. all-purpose flour
1/3 c. cornstarch
oil for deep frying
16-oz. pkg. mozzarella cheese
    sticks

In a bowl, beat together eggs and water. In a separate bowl, mix together bread crumbs and seasonings. Sift together flour and cornstarch in another bowl. Heat several inches of oil to 375 degrees in a saucepan over medium-high heat. Coat each mozzarella stick in flour mixture, then egg mixture, then bread crumb mixture. Fry sticks, a few at a time in hot oil, until golden, about 30 seconds to one minute. Drain on paper towels. Serves 8.

Nighttime football games can be chilly...stitch together a fleece lap blanket in team colors to keep cozy & warm. Fleece doesn't need hemming around the edges, so it couldn't be easier!

Pimento Cheese Spread

Ruth Kaup
Springfield, MO

This spread can be made ahead of time to have on hand for
unexpected guests or as a quick appetizer for holiday get-togethers.
It is delicious with crackers, party bread or raw vegetables.

16-oz. pkg. finely shredded
   Cheddar cheese
2 8-oz. pkgs. cream cheese,
   softened
2 T. sugar

1 t. onion powder
1/2 t. salt
1/2 t. pepper
4-oz. jar pimentos, drained
2 c. mayonnaise

Place all ingredients in a food processor; blend until smooth. To store,
cover and refrigerate. Serves 10 to 15.

Spinach & Artichoke Dip

Janice Ertola
Martinez, CA

This is the most delicious dip ever. I am asked to bring it
to every occasion I go to!

14-oz. can artichoke hearts in
   water, drained and chopped
10-oz. pkg. frozen chopped
   spinach, thawed and drained
1/8 c. Italian-flavored dry bread
   crumbs

1 c. mayonnaise
1/2 c. grated Parmesan cheese
1/2 t. garlic, minced
1/2 t. pepper
tortilla chips

Combine all ingredients in a large bowl; stir to mix well. Spoon
mixture into a lightly greased 8"x8" baking pan. Bake, uncovered,
at 400 degrees for 8 to 10 minutes, or until bubbly. Serve with tortilla
chips for dipping. Makes 4 to 6 servings.

Old-fashioned games are terrific ice-breakers at parties...
why not round up everyone at your next game-day get-together
for croquet or badminton?

MAJOR LEAGUE
Munchies

Hot Hamburger Dip

Sheryl Eastman
Wixom, MI

*My best friend gave me this recipe, and it's been a hit
every time I've made it.*

1 lb. ground beef
1/2 c. onion, chopped
8-oz. can tomato sauce
1/4 c. catsup
8-oz. pkg. cream cheese, cubed
1/2 c. grated Parmesan cheese

1 clove garlic, minced
1 t. dried oregano
1 t. sugar
salt and pepper to taste
tortilla chips or corn chips

Brown beef in a skillet over medium heat; drain. Add onion to beef and
cook until translucent. Stir in remaining ingredients except chips; cover.
Reduce heat to low and cook, stirring occasionally, until cream cheese is
melted. Serve with chips for dipping. Serves 8 to 10.

Awesome Dip

Brandi Killian
Coldwater, MI

*This is a family slow-cooker recipe passed down through the
generations. We enjoy it as an appetizer at our tailgate parties,
camping trips and any other events.*

1 lb. ground beef
16-oz. pkg. pasteurized process
    cheese spread, diced

16-oz. bottle salsa
tortilla chips

Brown beef in a skillet over medium heat; drain and spoon into a slow
cooker. Add cheese and salsa. Cover and cook on low setting, stirring
occasionally, for 4 hours, or until cheese is melted. Serve with tortilla
chips for dipping. Serves 8 to 10.

Grandma's Polish "Pizza"

Betty Kass
Fort Worth, TX

My precious mother-in-law came to visit us from Milwaukee for a couple of weeks, and ended up staying for six glorious months! She entertained all my family with her cooking. This is only one of many delectable items she made for us to enjoy.

8-oz. pkg. cream cheese, softened
8-oz. container sour cream
1-1/4 oz. pkg. taco seasoning mix
1 head lettuce, torn
1 tomato, diced
1 onion, diced
1 cucumber, diced
1 green pepper, diced
2 green onions, sliced
2 2-1/4 oz. cans sliced black olives, drained
8-oz. pkg. shredded Cheddar cheese
chips or crackers

Spread cream cheese evenly on a lightly greased 15" round pizza pan. In a bowl, mix together sour cream and taco seasoning; spread over cream cheese. Layer vegetables in order given over sour cream layer. Sprinkle evenly with cheese. Serve with chips or crackers for dipping. Serves 6 to 8.

Keep cutting boards smelling fresh by simply rubbing them thoroughly with lemon wedges...it works for hands too!

MAJOR LEAGUE
Munchies

Pepperoni Roll-ups

Nancy Girard
Chesapeake, VA

Wonderful for game-day noshing, this easy recipe would be equally tasty for lunch or a quick dinner with soup or a salad.

8-oz. tube refrigerated crescent
  rolls
16 slices pepperoni, quartered
2 mozzarella cheese sticks,
  quartered

3/4 t. Italian seasoning, divided
1/4 t. garlic salt, divided
Garnish: pizza sauce, warmed

Separate crescent roll dough into 8 triangles. Place 8 quartered pepperoni pieces on each triangle. Place a piece of string cheese on the long edge of each triangle; sprinkle with Italian seasoning. Starting with the long edge, roll up dough. Sprinkle rolls with garlic salt and remaining Italian seasoning. Place seam-side down, 2 inches apart on a lightly greased baking sheet. Bake at 375 degrees for 10 to 12 minutes, until golden. Serve with warmed pizza sauce for dipping. Makes 8.

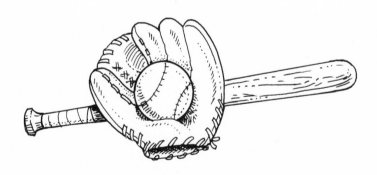

The way I figured it, I was even with baseball
and baseball with me. The game had done
much for me, and I had done much for it.

–Jackie Robinson

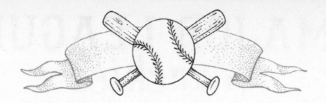

The Best Bruschetta

Heather Moses
Amherst, VA

This is the best bruschetta ever! My family loves it. We cannot wait until tomatoes are in season, and I grow my own basil so it's super fresh. Add some pasta salad on the side and you have an entire meal.

3 tomatoes, chopped
2 T. fresh basil, chopped
1 T. balsamic vinegar
2 T. olive oil
1 clove garlic, minced

1/2 t. pepper
1 loaf French bread, thinly sliced
Garnish: shredded Parmesan
   cheese

In a bowl, mix together all ingredients except bread and garnish. Cover and refrigerate for one hour to overnight to allow flavors to blend. At serving time, broil bread slices until golden. Top slices evenly with tomato mixture; sprinkle with cheese. Return bread slices to broiler until cheese melts. Serves 6 to 8.

Give slices of bruschetta some zip by using flavored olive oils.
Check the grocer for garlic, chili pepper, basil or even
black truffle-flavored oils!

MAJOR LEAGUE
Munchies

Party Pizza Bites

Linda Lundmark
Martinton, IL

I have made these tasty little party pizzas for many occasions over the years. They are so easy to prepare, even children can help make them.

3/4 lb. ground Italian pork
   sausage
6-oz. can tomato paste
1 T. dried, minced onion
1 t. Italian seasoning

1/2 t. salt
16-oz. pkg. phyllo dough,
   thawed
3/4 c. shredded mozzarella
   cheese

Brown sausage in a skillet over medium heat; drain. Stir in tomato paste, onion and seasonings; simmer for 5 minutes. Roll out one sheet phyllo dough, saving the rest for another recipe; cut out twelve, 3-inch circles. Spray muffin tins with non-stick vegetable spray. Press each circle into a muffin cup, to fit bottom and up the sides of cup. Add 1/4 cup sausage mixture to each cup; sprinkle with cheese. Bake at 400 degrees for 12 minutes, or until golden and cheese melts. Makes one dozen.

No tickets to the big game? Have a tailgate party anyway! Soak up the atmosphere by going to a local high school pep rally or pre-game party. Wear the team colors and cheer them on!

Verne's East Texas Salsa

Verne Sprott
Livingston, TX

*Everything's bigger in Texas, and the flavor of this salsa is no
exception. The cumin, cayenne pepper and jalapeño really add a
Texas-sized kick! Of course, you can always make it less spicy by
leaving out the cayenne.*

1 jalapeño pepper, halved and
    seeded
1 onion, quartered
2 cloves garlic
juice of 2 limes
1/2 c. fresh cilantro
1 T. cayenne pepper

1 t. ground cumin
1/2 t. salt
6 tomatoes, quartered
assorted dippers such as tortilla
    chips, corn chips, sliced
    cucumbers, sliced celery and
    sliced jicama

Place all ingredients except tomatoes and dippers in a food processor;
process until finely chopped. Add tomatoes and process again until just
chunky. Transfer salsa to a bowl; cover and refrigerate for at least
one hour to allow flavors to blend. Serve with dippers. Makes 15 to
18 servings.

For a super-simple appetizer that comes together in a flash,
just soften 8-ounce block of cream cheese and pour salsa
over the top. Serve with tortilla chips and crackers.

MAJOR LEAGUE
Munchies

Caramelized Onion Dip

JoAnn

I love caramelized onions on just about anything...soup, sandwiches, salads, pasta, you name it. So one day I though I'd whip up a dip that captured the sweet and savory flavors of caramelized onions. Needless to say, it was a hit with everyone!

4 t. olive oil
4 onions, diced
salt to taste
3 T. water
1-1/2 c. non-fat plain Greek
    yogurt
1/2 c. sour cream

2 T. lemon juice
1/4 t. cayenne pepper
Garnish: additional cayenne
    pepper
assorted dippers such as carrots,
    celery and radishes

Heat oil in a large non-stick skillet over medium heat. Cook and stir onions and salt in oil until golden and caramelized, about 35 to 40 minutes. Add water; cook and stir, scraping up any browned bits on the bottom of the skillet. Transfer onion mixture to a bowl; let stand 30 minutes. Mix in remaining ingredients except garnish. Cover and refrigerate for at least one hour to allow flavors to blend. Sprinkle with extra cayenne pepper before serving. Serve with assorted dippers. Serves 12.

Try serving "light" dippers with hearty full-flavored dips and spreads. Fresh veggies, pita wedges, baked tortilla chips and multi-grain crispbread are all sturdy enough to scoop yet won't overshadow the flavor of the dip.

Pecan-Crusted Salmon Ball

Deborah Jones
Benbrook, TX

This was the very first recipe that my husband's grandmother shared with me. It's delicious!

7-3/4 oz. can salmon, drained
　and flaked
8-oz. pkg. cream cheese,
　softened
2 t. Worcestershire sauce
1 t. smoke-flavored cooking
　sauce
2 green onions, chopped

1/2 c. green pepper, diced
1/2 c. black olives, chopped
2 c. shredded sharp Cheddar
　cheese
minced garlic to taste
Garnish: chopped pecans,
　chopped fresh parsley
assorted crackers

In a bowl, combine all ingredients except garnish and crackers; mix well. Cover and refrigerate for 4 hours. Meanwhile, combine pecans and parsley on a plate. Shape salmon mixture into a ball; roll in pecan mixture to coat. Serve with crackers for dipping. Serves 10.

Single servings! Roll Pecan-Crusted Salmon Ball into mini balls and place in paper muffin cups. Fill more paper muffin cups with crackers and pretzels and arrange alongside mini cheese balls.

MAJOR LEAGUE
Munchies

Nutty Cheese-Stuffed Celery

Kelly Alderson
Erie, PA

Not only are these super for game-day snacking, but I pack them with my lunch to take to work for a satisfying, mid-morning snack...so tasty.

2 8-oz. pkgs. cream cheese,
   softened
2 T. milk
1 T. Worcestershire sauce
1-1/3 c. chopped walnuts

1/2 t. onion salt
1/2 t. pepper
1 bunch celery, trimmed and cut
   into stalks

In a bowl, combine cream cheese, milk and Worcestershire sauce. Beat with an electric mixer on medium speed for 2 minutes until smooth. Stir in remaining ingredients except celery. Fill each piece of celery with filling; cut stalks into 2-1/2 to 3-inch pieces. Arrange on a serving platter. Refrigerate until ready to serve. Makes about 3-1/2 dozen pieces.

The secret to being a relaxed hostess...choose foods that can be prepared in advance. At party time, simply pull from the fridge and serve, or pop into a hot oven as needed.

Stuffed Pepperoncini

Judy Couto
Kerman, CA

*This is my own unique version of jalapeño poppers...
my family loves them!*

3 slices bacon
2 shallots, minced
1/2 red pepper, minced
3-oz. pkg. cream cheese,
    softened

2 T. milk
2 10-oz. jars pepperoncini,
    drained and peppers halved

In a skillet over medium heat, cook bacon until crisp; drain, reserving
2 tablespoons drippings in pan. Sauté shallots and red pepper in
drippings until tender. In a bowl, beat together cream cheese and milk
until smooth; stir in bacon and shallot mixture. Spoon mixture into a
plastic zipping bag. Snip off a corner of the bag and pipe filling into
pepper halves. Refrigerate peppers one to 2 hours, until set. Let stand
one hour at room temperature before serving. Makes about 2-1/2 dozen.

Fast & Easy Meatballs

Marsha Risafi
Las Vegas, NV

This is my most requested potluck recipe!

24-oz. pkg. frozen meatballs
1.35-oz. pkg. onion soup mix

12-oz. bottle beer or
    non-alcoholic beer

In a large saucepan over medium-high heat, combine all ingredients.
Bring to a boil; reduce heat to medium-low. Simmer until meatballs are
heated through, about 20 to 25 minutes. Serves 8.

SOUPER-BOWL
Soups, Salads & Sandwiches

Pulled Pork Sammies

Barbara Cissell
Louisville, KY

I've used a variety of colas in this slow-cooker recipe...each adds its own unique flavor. The best part is you can forget about these sammies and do other things while they cook.

3 to 5-lb. Boston butt pork roast
28-oz. can fire-roasted diced
   tomatoes
2 12-oz. cans cola

1-1/2 c. brown sugar, packed
3 T. chili powder
12 sandwich buns, split

Place pork in a slow cooker; add remaining ingredients except buns. Cover and cook on low setting for 8 hours, stirring occasionally, until pork is very tender. Shred pork with 2 forks; serve on buns with sauce from slow cooker. Serves 10 to 12.

Hole-In-One Pimento-Cheese Sandwiches

Sandra Sullivan
Aurora, CO

While baseball games have hot dogs, The Masters' golf tournament has pimento-cheese sandwiches...they're a tradition! My family enjoys them with a hot & hearty soup.

2 c. shredded extra-sharp
   Cheddar cheese
1/2 c. mayonnaise
3 T. pimentos, chopped
2 T. onion, grated

1 t. mustard
1/8 t. cayenne pepper
salt and pepper to taste
8 slices white bread

Combine all ingredients except bread in a bowl; mix until well blended. Divide mixture evenly among 4 slices of bread; top with remaining slices of bread. Cheese mixture will keep for 7 to 10 days refrigerated. Makes 4 sandwiches.

SOUPER-BOWL
Soups, Salads & Sandwiches

Beer-Cheese Soup

Holly Smith
Shaker Heights, OH

This is a favorite at our house during football season. Make it for lunch on a chilly autumn day...it will really warm you to your toes! It's just as tasty the next day too, if not tastier.

3 T. butter
1 onion, finely chopped
1 carrot, peeled and finely
   chopped
1 stalk celery, finely chopped
Optional: 1 jalapeño pepper,
   seeded and chopped
3 T. all-purpose flour
1 c. chicken broth
2 c. milk or half-and-half

2 c. shredded extra-sharp
   Cheddar cheese
1/2 c. beer or non-alcoholic beer,
   at room temperature
1/8 t. cayenne pepper
1/4 t. salt
1/4 t. pepper
Garnish: 2 T. green onions,
   chopped

Melt butter in a large saucepan over medium heat. Add onion, carrot, celery and jalapeño, if using; sauté until vegetables are crisp-tender. Add flour to vegetable mixture; stir well. In a small saucepan over medium heat, combine broth and milk or half-and-half; heat through. Pour broth mixture into vegetable mixture. Reduce heat to low and simmer, stirring occasionally, until soup begins to thicken, about 4 to 5 minutes. Stir in cheese and beer until cheese is completely melted. Stir in spices. Garnish with chopped green onions. Makes 4 servings.

Beer-Cheese Soup is traditionally topped with popcorn. Make it extra-cheesy and top a bowl with some cheesy popcorn...yum!

Crunchy Oriental Coleslaw

Carolyn Gulley
Cumberland Gap, TN

A friend wrote this recipe on the back of a church bulletin, and that's where I still read it from.

16-oz. pkg. coleslaw mix
3-oz. pkg. Oriental-flavored
   ramen noodles, uncooked
   and broken, seasoning packet
   reserved

1/4 c. slivered almonds, toasted
1/4 c. sunflower kernels
1/4 c. vinegar
1/2 c. sugar
1/2 c. olive or canola oil

In a large bowl, mix together coleslaw mix, broken noodles, almonds and sunflower kernels. In a separate small bowl, whisk together vinegar, sugar, oil and seasoning packet from noodles. Pour vinegar mixture over coleslaw mixture; toss before serving. Serves 8 to 10.

Mashed Potato Salad

Jo-Anne Bougie
Ontario, Canada

This is the most delicious potato salad I've ever tasted.

6 russet potatoes, peeled
1/2 c. mayonnaise
1/2 c. sour cream
1/2 t. sea salt
1/4 t. pepper
1 lb. cooked ham, chopped

2 eggs, hard-boiled, peeled and
   chopped
Garnish: sliced radishes, chopped
   green onions, shredded
   lettuce

Cover potatoes with water in a large stockpot over medium-high heat. Boil potatoes for 20 minutes, or until fork-tender; drain. Mash potatoes in stockpot, leaving a little lumpy; stir in mayonnaise, sour cream, salt and pepper. Fold in ham and eggs; garnish as desired. Serves 6.

Redskin Potato Salad

Sharon Dennison
Floyds Knobs, IN

This recipe is very similar to a potato salad that is served at
a local BBQ restaurant...it is amazing! I was told mine tastes exactly
like the restaurant's version, and that's a great compliment.

3 lbs. redskin potatoes
1-1/2 c. mayonnaise
2 T. milk
2 T. vinegar
1/2 t. salt
1/4 t. pepper

4 eggs, hard-boiled, peeled
   and diced
1 c. celery, sliced
1 t. celery seed
1/2 c. green onions, sliced

Cover potatoes with water in a large stockpot over medium-high heat.
Boil potatoes for 15 minutes, or until fork-tender. Drain and set aside to
cool. Meanwhile, whisk together mayonnaise, milk, vinegar, salt and
pepper in a small bowl; set aside. Once potatoes are cool, cut into
one-inch cubes; transfer to a large serving bowl. Pour mayonnaise
mixture over potatoes; fold in remaining ingredients. Cover and
refrigerate for 2 hours. Stir again before serving. Makes 10 to
12 servings.

Tote creamy salads to game-day get-togethers the no-spill way...
packed in a large plastic zipping bag. When you arrive,
simply pour the salad into a serving bowl.

Slow-Cooker Cheesesteak Sandwiches

Kristy Still
Broken Arrow, OK

Cut these sandwiches in half to make mini cheesesteak sandwiches!

1 lb. beef round steak, thinly
    sliced
1/2 onion, diced
1 red pepper, diced
1-1/2 t. garlic powder
1 T. butter

1 T. Worcestershire sauce
1 cube beef bouillon
16-oz. pkg. shredded Colby Jack
    cheese
4 hoagie rolls, split

Add all ingredients except cheese and rolls to a lightly greased slow cooker. Pour in enough water to just cover the ingredients. Cover and cook on low setting for 6 to 8 hours. Using a slotted spoon, place a serving of steak mixture on the bottom of each roll; sprinkle with cheese. Replace tops of rolls to make sandwiches. Makes 4 sandwiches.

Saucy sandwiches are best served on a vintage-style oilcloth...
spills wipe right up! Look for one with a colorful design of fruit,
flowers or even in your favorite team's colors!

6-Pack Texas Stew

Janine Edwards-Klinker
Gordonville, TX

This is the best stew I've ever eaten, and all my friends who have tried it agree! Served with crusty homemade bread, this hearty stew will fill you up and never let you down.

1-1/2 lbs. stew beef cubes
1/3 c. bacon, finely chopped
1 onion, chopped
3 T. paprika
1 T. salt
1 t. dried marjoram
2 12-oz. cans beer or
    non-alcoholic beer

1 c. water
8-oz. can tomato sauce
1 T. Worcestershire sauce
4 potatoes, cubed
1-1/2 c. baby carrots, sliced
1-1/2 c. turnips, peeled and
    sliced

Brown beef and bacon in a large stockpot over medium heat. Remove meat from pot and drain, leaving one tablespoon drippings. Add onion to drippings and cook until translucent. Return meat to pot and add seasonings, beer, water and sauces; stir to combine. Reduce heat to low; cover and simmer until beef is very tender, about 1-1/2 hours. Add vegetables to stockpot; cover and simmer until vegetables are tender, about 45 additional minutes. Serves 6 to 8.

Oops! If a soup or stew begins to burn on the bottom, all is not lost. Spoon it into another pan, being careful not to scrape up the scorched food on the bottom. The burnt taste usually won't linger.

Unstuffed Green Pepper Soup

Berta Campbell
Flint, MI

All the tangy, mouthwatering flavors of stuffed peppers, only in a soup! This recipe makes a lot, so it's perfect to whip up before having your family & friends over to watch the big game.

1-1/2 lbs. ground turkey
3 green peppers, chopped
1 onion, chopped
2 cloves garlic, minced
2 14-1/2 oz. cans tomato soup

2 14-1/2 oz. cans low-sodium
  beef broth
28-oz. can crushed tomatoes
1-1/2 c. cooked brown rice

In a large stockpot over medium heat, brown turkey with peppers, onion and garlic; drain. Stir in soup, broth and crushed tomatoes with juice; bring to a boil. Reduce heat to low. Cover and simmer until slightly thickened, about 30 minutes. Stir in rice just before serving. Serves 10.

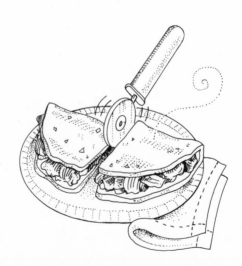

Quesadillas are quick and filling partners for a bowl of soup!
Sprinkle a flour tortilla with shredded cheese, top with
another tortilla and microwave on high until the cheese
melts. Cut into wedges and serve with salsa.

Spicy Italian Sausage Subs

Roxanne Sulzbach
Akron, OH

I made these sausage subs for my son's graduation party, and all his friends devoured them. Now I make them for just about any large get-together, and they're always a hit.

6 hot Italian pork sausage links
2 red peppers, sliced
1 green pepper, sliced
1 sweet onion, sliced

Optional: 14-1/2 oz. can diced
   tomatoes, drained
6 sub buns, split

Add sausage links to a large skillet over medium heat. Cook until outsides of sausage are just browned; drain. Reduce heat to low; add peppers, onion and tomatoes, if using, to skillet. Cover and cook for about one hour, until vegetables are tender and sausage is cooked through. To serve, place a sausage on each bun and top with peppers and onion. Makes 6 servings.

Warm sandwich buns for a crowd...easy! Fill a roaster with buns, cover with heavy-duty aluminum foil and cut several slits in the foil. Top with several dampened paper towels and tightly cover with more foil. Place in a 250-degree oven for 20 minutes. Rolls will be hot and steamy.

Red Devil Franks

Sara Wright
Colorado Springs, CO

*My grandmother used to make these tasty franks for her father
in the 1940s. The sauce just can't be beat...it has such a
unique and delicious flavor!*

2 to 4 T. butter
1 c. onion, finely chopped
2 cloves garlic, chopped
1-1/2 T. Worcestershire sauce
1-1/2 T. mustard
1-1/2 t. sugar

1/2 t. salt
1/8 t. pepper
1/2 c. chili sauce
1 lb. hot dogs
hot dog buns, split

Melt butter in a skillet over medium heat. Cook onion and garlic in
butter until translucent. Add remaining ingredients except hot dogs and
buns to onion mixture; stir. Cook, stirring occasionally, until heated
through, about 5 minutes. Split hot dogs lengthwise and arrange in a
single layer in a broiler pan. Spoon sauce over hot dogs; broil until
bubbly, about 5 minutes. Serve hot dogs on buns, topped with sauce.
Makes 8 servings.

Pick up a stack of retro-style plastic burger baskets.
Lined with crisp paper napkins, they're still such fun
for serving hot dogs, burgers and fries.

SOUPER-BOWL
Soups, Salads & Sandwiches

Mom's Spaghetti Salad

Nichole Boomers
Lowell, MI

My mom made this dish for every family event while I was growing up. It is always so delicious, and we love the leftovers...if there are any!

16-oz. pkg. spaghetti, uncooked
16-oz. bottle zesty Italian salad
  dressing
1 sweet onion, chopped

2.62-oz. jar salad seasoning
3 tomatoes, chopped
1 to 2 green peppers, chopped

Cook spaghetti according to package directions; drain and rinse with cold water. Place spaghetti in a large bowl. Add salad dressing, onion and salad seasoning; mix well. Cover and refrigerate for at least 2 to 3 hours. Just before serving, fold in tomatoes and peppers. Serves 12.

Simple Pepper Slaw

Sandra Monroe
Preston, MD

This family-favorite recipe was handed down to me from my grandfather's family.

1 c. white vinegar
1 c. water
1 c. sugar
1 t. celery seed

1 t. mustard seed
1 head cabbage, shredded
1 green pepper, chopped

In a saucepan over medium-high heat, combine vinegar, water, sugar, celery seed and mustard seed. Bring to a boil and cook for 5 minutes. Remove from heat and let cool completely. Meanwhile, combine cabbage and pepper in a large bowl. Pour cooled vinegar mixture over cabbage mixture; stir to coat well. Cover and refrigerate for 2 to 3 hours; stir again before serving. Makes 8 servings.

Chicken-Bacon Quesadilla

Karen Brice
Bethlehem, PA

The is the perfect one-pan appetizer or meal. It can't get any better than chicken, bacon and cheese! Cook up a couple for your next get-together and watch them disappear.

3 to 4 slices bacon
1/2 c. cooked chicken, diced
1 T. onion, chopped
1 T. green pepper, diced

2 10-inch flour tortillas
3/4 c. shredded Mexican-blend cheese, divided

In a large skillet, cook bacon until crisp; crumble and drain on paper towels. To same skillet, add chicken, onion and pepper; cook until vegetables are crisp-tender and chicken is warmed through. Place one tortilla in a separate ungreased skillet over medium heat; top with half the cheese. Place chicken mixture and bacon on top of cheese; top with remaining cheese and remaining tortilla. Cook until cheese begins to melt and bottom tortilla is crisp. Flip and cook other side until crisp, about 5 minutes. Remove from pan and cut into wedges to serve. Serves 2 to 4.

Put your pizza cutter to work full-time. It's perfect for cutting tortillas into strips and slicing cheesy quesadillas into wedges...you're sure to discover other uses!

SOUPER-BOWL
Soups, Salads & Sandwiches

Michelle's Spicy Vegetarian Chili

Cynthia Dodge
Layton, UT

We are a military family, and I love to collect recipes from the places we have lived. This recipe is from a very special neighbor, Michelle. Every time we serve this, someone always says, "Oh, good, we're having Michelle's chili!"

2 T. olive oil
1 onion, chopped
1-1/2 c. frozen tri-colored sliced peppers, chopped
1 T. garlic, minced
1-1/4 oz. pkg. taco seasoning mix
1 t. ground cumin
28-oz. can diced tomatoes

15-oz. can black-eyed peas
15-oz. can black beans
Optional: 15-oz. can garbanzo beans
1 c. fresh or frozen corn
11-oz. pkg. fresh baby spinach
2 T. lemon juice
Garnish: sour cream

Heat oil in a large Dutch oven over medium heat. Sauté onion, peppers and garlic in oil until tender, about 6 to 8 minutes. Add taco seasoning and cumin to onion mixture; mix well and cook for an additional minute. Add undrained tomatoes and all undrained beans. Stir to mix; add frozen corn. Simmer for about 10 minutes, until corn is heated through. Remove from heat; fold in spinach and lemon juice. Cover and let stand 5 minutes to wilt spinach. Top individual servings with a dollop of sour cream. Serves 6 to 8.

There's no such thing as too much chili! Top hot dogs and baked potatoes with extra chili. You can even spoon chili into flour tortillas and sprinkle with shredded cheese for quick burritos.

White Chicken Chili

Cherilyn Dunn
Fairborn, OH

We have one daughter and five hungry sons. This is a scrumptious and easy slow-cooker soup that satisfies my active family's appetite...it's their favorite chili!

4 boneless, skinless chicken breasts
6 15-1/2 oz. cans Great Northern beans
2 4-oz. cans chopped green chiles
4 c. chicken broth
2 onions, diced
2 t. ground cumin
1-1/2 t. garlic, minced
1-1/2 t. dried oregano
1/2 t. white pepper
1/4 t. cayenne pepper
24-oz. container sour cream

Place all ingredients except sour cream in a slow cooker; do not drain beans or chiles. Cover and cook on low setting for 6 to 8 hours, until chicken is cooked through. Remove chicken from chili and dice; return to slow cooker. Stir in sour cream just before serving. Makes 12 servings.

Crunchy toppings can really add fun and flavor to chili or soup. Some fun choices...fish-shaped crackers, bacon bits, French fried onions, sunflower seeds or toasted nuts.

Zesty Chicken Pasta Salad

Vicki Lanzendorf
Madison, WI

This tangy pasta salad is perfect on those hot summer days when you don't want to heat up the kitchen by using the oven. It's also a breeze when you're short on time because it comes together in a flash!

1 c. light mayonnaise-type salad
    dressing
1/2 c. orange juice
2 t. dried basil
1/4 t. ground ginger
2 c. rotini pasta, cooked

4 boneless, skinless chicken
    breasts, cooked and cubed
11-oz. can mandarin oranges,
    drained
1/2 c. chopped pecans

In a bowl, whisk together salad dressing, juice, basil and ginger. Add remaining ingredients; mix well. Cover and refrigerate for at least 2 hours to allow flavors to blend. Stir again before serving. Serves 6.

Pasta salad is so versatile and works well with just about any veggies on hand. Toss in chopped celery, cucumbers, grated carrots or even cheese chunks for a new dish every time.

Sweet & Salty Pretzel Salad

Christina Manzer
Satellite Beach, FL

My mother-in-law passed this recipe down to me. This versatile and yummy salad can be used as a dessert or side dish. It is always a hit at our family gatherings.

2 c. pretzels, crushed
1 c. plus 3 T. sugar, divided
1 c. butter, melted
3 8-oz. pkgs. cream cheese, softened
8-oz. container frozen whipped topping, thawed

2 3-oz. pkgs. strawberry gelatin mix
2 c. boiling water
2 10-oz. pkgs. frozen sweetened strawberries, partially thawed

In a bowl, combine crushed pretzels, 3 tablespoons sugar and butter; mix well. Press into a 13"x9" baking pan. Bake at 350 degrees for 8 to 10 minutes, until golden. Let cool completely. Meanwhile, in a separate bowl, combine cream cheese, whipped topping and remaining sugar. Beat with an electric mixer on medium speed for 3 to 5 minutes, until smooth. Spread cream cheese mixture evenly over cooled pretzel crust; refrigerate. Meanwhile, in a bowl, combine dry gelatin mixes and water; stir until mixes are dissolved, about 2 minutes. Add strawberries to gelatin mixture; stir well and let stand 10 minutes until partially set. Pour strawberry mixture over cream cheese layer. Cover and chill until ready to serve. Serves 16.

Turn chocolate-dipped strawberries into tasty little footballs!
Pipe melted white chocolate onto strawberries for
the lacing and details...so cute.

Colossal Italian Sandwich

Louise Graybiel
Ontario, Canada

This GIANT sandwich is perfect for having friends over...it's super-easy. Plus, there are some spectacular Italian flavors. You don't usually find artichoke hearts on sandwiches, but their taste is amazing.

8-inch round loaf foccacia bread
2 T. garlic spread
2 T. Italian salad dressing
1/4 c. green olives, chopped
1/4 c. black olives, chopped
1/2 c. marinated artichoke
    hearts, drained and chopped

8 slices salami
8 slices provolone cheese
8 slices prosciutto ham
8 slices mozzarella cheese
8 slices mortadella sausage
8 slices Asiago cheese
3 roasted red peppers, sliced

Slice bread loaf in half horizontally. Spread top half with garlic spread and bottom half with salad dressing. Sprinkle bottom half of loaf with chopped olives and artichoke hearts. Layer remaining ingredients in order given. Replace top half of bread loaf; slice to serve. Serves 4 to 6.

White paper coffee filters make tidy toss-away holders
for hot dog buns, sandwiches or tacos.

Cakewich

Polly McCallum
Palatka, FL

For something just a little different, I made this for a dessert auction we had at our church. Needless to say, it was a huge hit, plus it brought in $80! Not bad, if I do say so myself.

1 loaf sliced honey wheat bread
8-oz. pkg. thinly sliced deli
   turkey
6 slices provolone cheese
1/4 c. mustard
1/2 c. sliced pickles
9-oz. pkg. thinly sliced deli ham
6 slices Swiss cheese

1/4 head lettuce, shredded
3 slices tomato
7-oz. pkg. thinly sliced roast beef
6 slices Pepper Jack cheese
1/4 c. spicy mustard
1/4 c. mayonnaise
Garnish: 8 olives

Press 5 slices of bread in a single layer into the bottom of a 10" round springform pan. Layer turkey, provolone cheese, mustard and pickles on top of bread. Top pickles with another 5 slices of bread. Layer ham, Swiss cheese, lettuce and tomato on top of second bread layer. Press another 5 slices of bread on top of tomatoes. Layer roast beef, Pepper Jack cheese, and spicy mustard on top of third bread layer. Top with 5 more bread slices. Release springform pan and remove cake to a serving plate; spread top with mayonnaise to resemble frosting. Garnish with olives. Cut into slices to serve. Serves 10.

If you're making a sandwich several hours before serving first spread a light layer of softened butter on the bread. This prevents the bread from absorbing the moisture from the filling and becoming soggy.

SOUPER-BOWL
Soups, Salads & Sandwiches

Ditalini Nicoline Soup

JoAnna Nicoline-Haughey
Berwyn, PA

*I came up with the name because my last name
rhymed with the type of pasta I used!*

2 32-oz. containers vegetable
   broth
12-oz. pkg. steam-in-bag leaf
   spinach
1-1/2 c. ditalini pasta, uncooked

14-1/2 oz. can seasoned diced
   tomatoes
5 slices bacon, crisply cooked
   and crumbled
1/2 c. grated Parmesan cheese

In a large stockpot over medium-high heat, bring broth to a boil.
Meanwhile, steam spinach according to package directions. Add spinach
and remaining ingredients to broth. Cook for 12 minutes, or until pasta
is tender. Makes 6 servings.

Caprese Pasta Salad

Laura Fullen
Fort Wayne, IN

*The classic light Italian salad spruced up with some pasta,
basil and lots of cheese!*

1 c. fresh basil
1/4 c. grated Romano cheese
1/4 c. pine nuts
2 cloves garlic
1/4 c. olive oil
16-oz. pkg. fusilli pasta, cooked

1 pt. cherry tomatoes, halved
2 T. grated Parmesan cheese
4-oz. ball fresh mozzarella
   cheese, cut into strips
salt and pepper to taste

Place basil, Romano cheese, pine nuts and garlic in a food processor.
Pulse until mixture is a coarse paste. With food processor turned on, add
oil in a slow, steady stream, processing until smooth. In a large bowl,
combine cooked pasta, tomatoes, Parmesan cheese, mozzarella cheese
and pesto. Season with salt and pepper; mix well. Refrigerate, covered,
for 45 minutes; stir again before serving. Serves 8.

German Spiessbraten

Violet Leonard
Chesapeake, VA

I learned this recipe from a friend when we were living at Bitburg Air Base, Germany. This overnight dish is a perfect idea for a cookout if you're looking for something different from run-of-the-mill hamburgers and hot dogs.

3 T. salt
2 t. pepper
1-1/2 T. paprika
1-1/2 T. celery salt
1 T. garlic powder

4 t. meat tenderizer
1 onion, thinly sliced
5-lb. pork tenderloin, cut into
    serving-size pieces
12 crusty hard rolls, split

Combine all spices and tenderizer in a small bowl; set aside. Alternately layer onion and pork in a large lidded food container, sprinkling evenly with seasoning mixture after each layer. Cover and refrigerate for 24 hours. Grill pork and onion on a medium-hot grill until pork is no longer pink in the center and onion is tender. Serve pork and onion on split rolls. Makes 12 sandwiches.

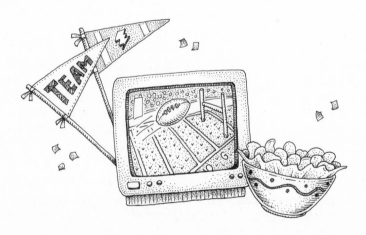

As you walk down the fairway of life you must smell the roses,
for you only get to play one round.

–Ben Hogan

SOUPER-BOWL
Soups, Salads & Sandwiches

White Cheddar-Ale Soup

Melissa Flasck
Sterling Heights, MI

My husband and I enjoyed this amazing soup on an anniversary trip. This is my effort to recreate it so we can enjoy it all the time. It is great for crisp autumn evenings before going to watch a high school football game.

2 T. butter
1 onion, diced
2 carrots, peeled and diced
4 cloves garlic, minced
1/3 c. all-purpose flour
1 c. ale or chicken broth
1 T. Worcestershire sauce
2 c. milk

2 c. chicken broth
8-oz. pkg. shredded sharp white
　　Cheddar cheese
1/2 to 1 c. shredded Swiss cheese
salt and pepper to taste
Garnish: crushed honey-mustard
　　and onion flavored pretzels
Optional: hot pepper sauce

Melt butter in a stockpot over medium heat. Sauté onion and carrots until softened, about 20 minutes. Add garlic to onion mixture; cook an additional minute. Add flour; cook, stirring constantly, for 3 to 4 minutes. Add ale or one cup broth and cook, stirring constantly, for 3 minutes. Stir in Worcestershire sauce, milk and 2 cups broth; simmer for 12 minutes. Purée soup in batches in a food processor. Return soup to pot and turn heat to medium-low. Add cheese, a handful at a time, stirring constantly until cheese has melted. Do not allow soup to boil. Season with salt and pepper. Garnish individual servings with crushed pretzels and hot sauce, if using. Serves 6.

Stir up a loaf of beer bread to go with White Cheddar-Ale Soup. Combine 3 cups self-rising flour, a 12-ounce can of beer and 3 tablespoons sugar in a greased loaf pan. Bake for 25 minutes at 350 degrees, then drizzle with melted butter.

The Best Chicken & Corn Chowder

Mary Reif
Girard, KS

With a name like that, you can't help but try this savory, spicy chowder. Serve with some big squares of buttered cornbread and you've got yourself a hearty Tex-Mex meal!

3 T. butter
4 boneless, skinless chicken
  breasts, cooked and shredded
1/2 c. onion, chopped
2 cloves garlic
2 cubes chicken bouillon

1 c. hot water
2 c. half-and-half
2 c. shredded Montery Jack
  cheese
14-3/4 oz. can creamed corn
4-oz. can chopped green chiles

Melt butter in a large Dutch oven over medium heat. Cook chicken, onion and garlic in butter until chicken is heated through and onion is translucent, about 10 minutes. Meanwhile, dissolve bouillon cubes in hot water. Pour bouillon mixture into chicken mixture; bring to a boil. Reduce heat to medium-low; add remaining ingredients. Stir until cheese is completely melted. Makes 4 to 6 servings.

Soups are ideal for casual tailgating get-togethers. Borrow three or four slow cookers and fill each with a different soup, stew or chowder. Or, better yet, ask friends to bring their favorite soup to share!

SOUPER-BOWL
Soups, Salads & Sandwiches

Apple-Chicken Salad Sandwich

Linda Cook
Ontario, Canada

Many years ago, I used to work in downtown Toronto and I would frequent a certain sandwich shop. I loved its chicken salad sandwiches! I couldn't remember exactly what was in their chicken salad, but I think after a few tries I got pretty close.

1 boneless, skinless chicken
    breast, grilled and cubed
2 T. mayonnaise, or to taste
1 T. sunflower kernels
1 T. dried cranberries

1/2 red onion, chopped
1 apple, cored and cubed
salt and pepper to taste
2 sandwich buns, split

Combine all ingredients except buns in a large bowl; stir well. Place buns, split-side up, under a broiler to toast. Fill buns evenly with chicken mixture. Makes 2 sandwiches.

Pocket Sammies

Marni McDowell
Boise, ID

These warm, hand-held sandwiches are so much better than the store-bought version.

1 lb. ground beef
1/2 c. onion, diced
1 c. barbecue sauce

12 frozen dinner rolls, thawed
12 slices American cheese

In a skillet over medium heat, brown beef and onion; drain. Add barbecue sauce to beef mixture; simmer until thickened, about 5 minutes. Roll out each roll into a 6-inch round. Evenly divide beef mixture among dough rounds; top each with a slice of cheese. Fold over edges and crimp seams together with a fork. Place on a lightly greased baking sheet. Bake at 400 degrees for 15 minutes, or until golden. Makes 12 sandwiches.

Reuben Roll

Stephanie Dardani-D'Esposito
Ravena, NY

My dad used to make this sandwich roll for me on the weekends after softball games...it's so yummy. Try making it with pastrami too!

16-oz. pkg. frozen pizza dough, thawed
1 lb. thinly sliced deli corned beef
1/2 lb. sliced Swiss cheese

14-1/2 oz. can sauerkraut, drained
Optional: olive oil and garlic salt

Roll out dough into a 12-inch round. Evenly top dough with corned beef. Layer cheese over beef; sprinkle evenly with sauerkraut. Fold in 2 sides of the dough and roll up, sealing edges. Brush dough with olive oil and sprinkle with garlic salt, if desired. Place on a lightly greased baking sheet. Bake at 350 degrees for 35 to 45 minutes, until golden. Slice to serve. Makes 8 servings.

For a party or potluck, roll up sets of flatware in table napkins and place in a shallow tray. An easy do-ahead for the hostess...guests will find it simple to pull out individual sets too.

SOUPER-BOWL
Soups, Salads & Sandwiches

All-Season Coleslaw

Jo Ann Belovitch
Stratford, CT

This classic-style coleslaw is perfect any time of year, but I think it's best served with a grilled hot dog and some baked beans at a picnic or tailgating celebration.

1/2 c. mayonnaise
1/3 c. milk
1/4 c. sugar
1 t. vinegar

1/4 t. salt
1/4 t. pepper
16-oz. pkg. coleslaw mix

In a large bowl, combine all ingredients except coleslaw mix. Whisk together until smooth. Add coleslaw mix; toss well. Cover and refrigerate for at least one hour before serving. Serves 6 to 8.

Carolina-Style Slaw Dressing

Daryl Johnson
Lindstrom, MN

This dressing is tasty on just about any kind of salad, especially cabbage and carrot-based ones. We often enjoy it on a simple cucumber-tomato salad.

1 c. white vinegar
2-1/2 c. sugar
1 c. oil

1 onion, chopped
1-3/4 t. sea salt
1-3/4 t. celery salt

In a saucepan over medium-high heat, combine vinegar and sugar; bring to a boil. Cook and stir until sugar is dissolved. Remove from heat and let cool. Add remaining ingredients to vinegar mixture and transfer to a blender. Blend on high speed until smooth. Store in a jar with a tightly fitting lid. Makes one quart.

Spicy Cajun Potato Salad

Kay Little
Diana, TX

I started with my all-time favorite recipe for potato salad and just spiced up the dressing to make this spicy potato salad. I'm thinking about adding some crayfish tails the next time I make it...now that will be Cajun for sure!

5 lbs. Yukon Gold potatoes, peeled and cubed
1 T. salt
1/2 c. dill pickles, diced
1/2 onion, diced
8 green onions, thinly sliced
1-1/2 c. celery, diced
1 T. fresh parsley, coarsely chopped

1-1/2 to 1-3/4 c. mayonnaise
1/2 to 3/4 c. mustard
1 T. Cajun seasoning
1 t. pepper
2 eggs, hard-boiled, peeled and diced
Garnish: paprika

Place potatoes and salt in a large stockpot over medium-high heat; add enough water to just cover potatoes. Bring to a boil; cook potatoes for 15 minutes, or until fork-tender. Drain and transfer to a large bowl; cool. Lightly break up potatoes with a fork; stir in pickles, onions, celery and parsley. In a separate bowl, stir together mayonnaise, mustard and Cajun seasoning. Fold dressing into potato mixture; sprinkle with pepper. Gently fold in eggs. Garnish with paprika and refrigerate until serving time. Makes 10 to 12 servings.

To keep potato salads cold, freeze a stoneware bowl ahead of time. Just before leaving on your picnic, transfer salad into the bowl and cover with aluminum foil. This will keep the food colder for longer.

SOUPER-BOWL
Soups, Salads & Sandwiches

South Carolina Gumbo

Kristin Slaughter
Bartlesville, OK

The okra in this recipe imparts a rich flavor to the gumbo and aids in thickening it as it simmers. Add some crusty bread, and you've got yourself one heck of a meal!

1 T. olive oil
1 onion, chopped
1 stalk celery, sliced
1/2 green pepper, chopped
2 c. boneless, skinless chicken
  breasts, cubed
2 c. okra, chopped
2 14-1/2 oz. cans chicken broth

1 c. water
14-1/2 oz. can diced tomatoes,
  drained
2 t. Cajun seasoning
1/2 t. garlic powder
1 t. salt
1/2 t. pepper
1 c. instant rice, uncooked

Heat oil in a large stockpot over medium heat. Add onion, celery and green pepper to oil; sauté until tender, about 8 to 10 minutes. Add chicken and remaining ingredients except rice; bring to a boil. Reduce heat and simmer, covered, for 15 minutes, or until chicken is fully cooked. Add rice and simmer 15 more minutes, or until rice is tender. Serves 4 to 6.

Okra helps thicken soups and stews...it's tasty too!
When cut, the raw okra releases a syrupy liquid that thickens broths while it cooks.

Kick-It-Right Chili

Marcia Marcoux
Charlton, MA

This chili isn't super-hot, but feel free to amp it up for those who like their chili spicier by adding some diced jalapeños or some chipotle peppers in adobo sauce.

2 T. olive oil
1 lb. ground beef
1 onion, finely chopped
1 green pepper, finely chopped
3 cloves garlic, minced
14-1/2 oz. can stewed tomatoes
15-1/2 oz. can red kidney beans,
　drained and rinsed
15-1/2 oz. can black beans,
　drained and rinsed

1/4 c. tomato paste
1/4 c. honey
1 T. chili powder
1 t. ground cumin
1 t. dried oregano
1/2 t. salt
1/4 t. hot pepper sauce
Garnish: shredded Cheddar
　cheese, sliced green onions

Heat oil in a large Dutch oven over medium-high heat. Brown beef in oil. Add onion, green pepper and garlic to beef; cook for 5 minutes, or until vegetables are tender; drain. Add tomatoes with juice and remaining ingredients except garnish; reduce heat to medium-low. Simmer, covered, for 2 hours, stirring occasionally. Top individual servings with cheese and onions. Serves 4 to 6.

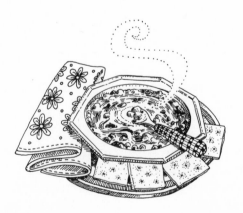

If your chili is too thick for your liking, just thin it out with some beef or chicken broth...if it's too thin, thicken it up by adding some tomato paste.

4-H Michigan Sauce

Chris Rivers
Hudson, NY

Growing up in northern New York, I become a fan of Michigans...a steamed hot dog slathered with a meaty tomato sauce. This is by far the best sauce; the recipe is from a long-gone stand that my parents would take me to as a treat.

3 lbs. ground beef
28-oz. can crushed tomatoes
28-oz. can tomato purée
1-1/4 oz. pkg. chili seasoning
    mix
1/4 c. catsup

1/4 c. mustard
1/3 c. brown sugar, packed
1 onion, chopped
1 clove garlic, chopped
1 T. Worcestershire sauce

Mix together uncooked beef, tomatoes with juice and remaining ingredients in a large stockpot. Mash with a potato masher until texture is very smooth. Place over medium-low heat. Simmer for about 2 to 3 hours, until beef is cooked through. Makes 18 to 20 servings.

Coney Dog Sauce

Brenda Huey
Geneva, IN

This sauce is excellent. My friend Vicki gave this recipe to me, and it tastes just like the hot dog sauce at root beer stands...it's wonderful!

2 lbs. ground beef
2/3 c. water
1/4 c. onion, finely chopped
4-1/2 t. chili powder

1/8 t. ground cumin
1/2 t. salt
2 c. catsup
2 t. cider vinegar

Combine uncooked beef and remaining ingredients except vinegar in a large stock pot over medium heat. Simmer, covered, for one hour, until beef is cooked through. Stir in vinegar before serving. Makes 12 servings.

Spicy Italian Sausage Stew

Erin Carnes
Gaines, MI

This is an absolutely awesome stew. The spicy sausage adds a lot of warmth on wintery Michigan days. As with most stews, it gets even tastier the next day! Serve with some warm homemade bread or garlic toast.

1-1/2 lb. spicy ground Italian pork sausage
2 onions, diced
1 green pepper, diced
4 cloves garlic, minced
6 c. chicken broth
28-oz. can diced tomatoes
1 c. ditalini pasta, uncooked
2 sprigs fresh rosemary
6-oz. pkg. fresh baby spinach
2 T. balsamic vinegar
1 t. salt
Garnish: grated Parmesan cheese

Brown sausage in a stockpot over medium heat. Drain on paper towels, reserving one tablespoon drippings in stockpot. Sauté onions and pepper in drippings until tender, about 8 minutes. Add garlic and cook an additional minute. Stir in sausage, broth, tomatoes with juice, pasta and rosemary. Bring to a simmer and cook 10 to 15 minutes, or until pasta is tender. Remove from heat; discard rosemary sprigs. Stir in spinach, vinegar and salt. Let stand for 2 to 3 minutes, until spinach is wilted. Top individual servings with cheese. Serves 8.

A hearty dish like Spicy Italian Sausage Stew is perfect on a cool autumn night. Carry the stockpot right out to your backyard picnic table and savor the fall colors with your family!

Italian Beef Dip Sandwiches

Robyn Stroh
Calera, AL

My family loves these sandwiches! They're great to take the chill off after a long winter day, and they're fun and easy to serve at a party. This recipe cooks in the oven while you're free to mingle and talk with your guests.

4-lb. beef chuck roast
0.7-oz. pkg. Italian salad
   dressing mix, divided
16-oz. jar pepperoncini peppers
   with juice
1 t. salt

1/2 c. water
2 10-1/2 oz. cans beef
   consommé or beef broth
10 to 12 hoagie or ciabatta rolls,
   split
10 to 12 slices provolone cheese

Place roast in a Dutch oven. Add remaining ingredients except rolls and cheese; stir to mix well. Bake, covered, at 325 degrees for 2-1/2 to 3 hours, until beef is very tender. Shred beef with 2 forks. Spoon some beef mixture onto the bottom half of a roll; top with a slice of cheese and top of roll. Bake sandwiches on a baking sheet at 400 degrees for 5 to 8 minutes, until cheese is melted and rolls are crisp. Serve sandwiches with some juice from the Dutch oven for dipping. Makes 10 to 12 sandwiches.

At your next dinner party, set out a guest book!
Ask everyone young and old to sign...it will become
a treasured journal of the occasion.

Sensational Sausage & Kale Soup

Jenny Wright
Carneys Point, NJ

*This delicious soup is similar to one I had in a restaurant once.
I liked it so well that I just had to recreate it...now I can
enjoy it whenever I want!*

10 c. water
5 cubes chicken bouillon
3 potatoes, diced
1 lb. ground Italian pork sausage
1-1/2 t. red pepper flakes
6 slices bacon, diced

1 onion, diced
2 t. garlic, minced
1 c. whipping cream
1 bunch kale, stems removed
　　and coarsely chopped

Place water, bouillon cubes and potatoes in a large stockpot over medium-high heat. Boil potatoes until tender, about 15 to 20 minutes; do not drain. Meanwhile, brown sausage and red pepper flakes in a skillet over medium heat; drain and set aside. In same skillet, cook bacon, onion and garlic until bacon is crisp and onion is soft; drain. Add bacon mixture and sausage mixture to stockpot. Stir in cream and heat through. Fold in kale and cook until just wilted. Serves 8 to 10.

Removing the tough stems from kale leaves is easy!
Just fold each leaf in half, then cut down the side
of the leaf the stem is on.

SLAM-DUNK
Mains & Sides

Race-Day Shredded Pork

Christina Miller
Delaware, OH

This is my husband's favorite take-along dish for his weekend racing trips! I prepare it the day before, and the next day he's got a heat & serve dish that's a huge crowd-pleaser.

3 to 4-lb. boneless pork shoulder
12-oz. can frozen apple juice
  concentrate, thawed

1/2 c. cider vinegar
12 to 16 sandwich rolls, split
Garnish: barbecue sauce

Rub pork on all sides with Dry Rub. Place in a large plastic zipping bag; refrigerate overnight. Place pork in a large slow cooker; top with apple juice and vinegar. Cover and cook on high setting for one hour; reduce heat to low setting. Continue to cook for 8 to 9 hours, until pork is very tender. Remove pork from slow cooker and let stand 15 minutes; shred with 2 forks. Serve pork on rolls with barbecue sauce. Makes 6 to 8 servings.

Dry Rub:

3 T. brown sugar, packed
1 T. salt
1 T. pepper
1 T. ground cumin
1 T. paprika

1 T. mesquite seasoning
1 T. garlic powder
1-1/2 t. cayenne pepper,
  or to taste

Mix together all ingredients in a bowl.

Turn your favorite shredded pork, beef or chicken barbecue recipe into a delicious appetizer. Serve up bite-size sandwiches using brown & serve rolls as mini buns.

SLAM-DUNK
Mains & Sides

Bar-B-Q Sliders

Helen Rose Smith
Woodbridge, NJ

These tasty little slider sandwiches are a big hit at game-day parties. You might want to double the recipe, because you guests will be coming back for more and more!

1 T. oil
1 onion, finely diced
2 cloves garlic, minced
2 lbs. deli chipped ham, diced

1 c. catsup
1 c. cola
24 Hawaiian sweet rolls, split
1 c. shredded Cheddar cheese

Heat oil in a skillet over medium heat. Sauté onion and garlic in oil until translucent; add ham. Cook, stirring occasionally, until ham is lightly golden. Add catsup and cola to ham mixture; simmer and stir until thickened. Meanwhile, arrange bottoms of rolls, sides touching, in a rimmed baking sheet. Spoon ham mixture evenly over bottoms of rolls; sprinkle cheese on top. Place pan under a broiler and broil until cheese melts, about 5 minutes. Add tops of rolls. Makes 2 dozen.

Just for fun, hold slider sandwiches together or serve meatballs with party toothpicks that have footballs or baseballs on them.

Bacon-Wrapped Corn on the Cob

Linda Stone
Cookeville, TN

You can get these tasty morsels ready the night before by refrigerating the ears in plastic zipping bags. Just take them out and toss on the grill...so easy!

8 ears corn, unhusked   1 lb. bacon

Soak corn for about 30 minutes in cold water. Remove corn from water; pull back husks and remove corn silk, leaving husks intact. Wrap 2 slices of bacon around each ear; pull husks back up around corn. Place ears on a hot grill, turning occasionally, until bacon is cooked and corn is tender, about 20 minutes. Makes 8 servings.

Creamy Bacon Corn-Fetti

Tammy Epperson
Nancy, KY

I love the taste of corn and bacon, so I whipped this up and couldn't be happier with the results...so yummy!

8 slices bacon   1/2 c. half-and-half
1 onion, chopped   1 t. sugar
1/3 c. green pepper, chopped   1 t. salt
4 15-1/4 oz. cans corn, drained   1 t. pepper
8-oz. pkg. cream cheese, cubed

In a skillet over medium heat, cook bacon until crisp. Drain, crumble and set aside, reserving 2 tablespoons drippings in skillet. Sauté onion, pepper and corn in drippings until crisp-tender. Reduce heat to low; stir in cream cheese and half-and-half. Cook, stirring occasionally, until cheese melts. Add sugar, salt and pepper; fold in bacon. Serves 8.

SLAM-DUNK
Mains & Sides

Heavenly Hot Dogs

Diana Jones
Landisburg, PA

I remember eating these hot dogs as a child on cold winter evenings. Now my children and their spouses love to come up and have this delicious, quick meal with me on a chilly evening.

8 hot dogs
3 c. mashed potatoes
1 c. shredded sharp Cheddar
   cheese

Garnish: paprika

Slice hot dogs lengthwise without cutting all the way through. Lay split hot dogs on an ungreased baking sheet. Spoon 3 tablespoons mashed potatoes into each hot dog. Sprinkle cheese evenly over mashed potatoes; garnish with paprika. Bake at 350 degrees for 30 minutes, or until cheese is melted and bubbly. Makes 4 servings.

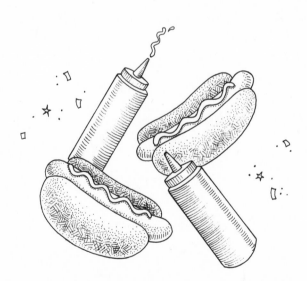

Economical and quick-cooking, hot dogs and smoked sausage are great choices for tailgating! Different flavors like hickory-smoked or cheese-filled can really jazz up a recipe too.

Old-Fashioned Corn Dogs

Sharry Murawski
Oak Forest, IL

You just can't beat a homemade corn dog! My mom used to make us these corn dogs when I was young. Now, I don't make them too often, but when the mood strikes...these really hit the spot.

1/2 c. cornmeal
1-1/2 c. all-purpose flour
4 t. baking powder
1 c. milk
2 t. salt

1/4 c. sugar
1 egg, beaten
8 hot dogs
8 wooden craft sticks
oil for deep frying

In a large bowl, mix together cornmeal, flour, baking powder, milk, salt, sugar and egg until smooth; set aside. Pat hot dogs dry. Insert a stick into each hot dog, leaving some exposed for a handle. Heat about 2 inches of oil to 365 degrees in a deep saucepan over medium-high heat. Roll hot dogs in batter until evenly coated. Fry hot dogs in oil, a few at a time, until golden on all sides. Drain on paper towels before serving. Makes 8.

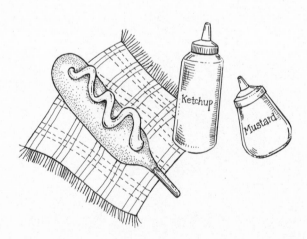

To help the batter stick to the hot dog, roll dry hot dogs in flour, making sure to shake off any excess, before dipping in the batter. This will give the batter something easier to stick to.

SLAM-DUNK
Mains & Sides

Walter's Smoky Potatoes

Lerri Blow
Jemison, AL

I was given this recipe by a sweet man I used to work with. I made it just like he said, and it was amazing. The potatoes come out so tender, plus the green pepper and onion add a wonderful taste to the dish. You can also place everything in foil packets and cook them on the grill.

8 to 10 baking potatoes, cubed
1 green pepper, diced
1 onion, diced
14-oz. smoked pork sausage
    ring, sliced

2 t. garlic powder
1/2 t. salt
1 t. pepper
10 T. butter, melted and divided

In a large bowl, combine potatoes, green pepper, onion and sausage. Sprinkle with garlic powder, salt and pepper. Add 5 tablespoons butter; mix well to coat. Fold in remaining butter. Transfer mixture to 2 lightly greased 8"x8" baking pans. Bake, covered, at 400 degrees for one hour, or until potatoes are tender. Serves 8 to 10.

A splash of ginger ale in orange juice makes a refreshing beverage to accompany a cookout meal. Serve in tall glasses with lots of ice...aah!

Curtis's Cheesy Creamy Twice-Baked Potatoes

Stacy Richardson
Hutchinson, KS

These potatoes are a hit with the family. Even picky eaters are quick to grab one up. Who could resist all the yummy cheese and bacon on these tasty spuds?

4 baking potatoes
sea salt to taste
8 slices bacon
1/2 c. sour cream
1/2 c. whipping cream
1/2 c. cream cheese, cubed
1/4 c. butter
1/2 t. salt
1/2 t. pepper

2 to 3 cloves garlic, minced
1/4 lb. Gouda cheese, diced
1/8 c. shredded Romano cheese
1/8 c. shredded Parmesan cheese
8 green onions, chopped and
   divided
1/2 c. shredded sharp Cheddar
   cheese, divided

After washing potatoes, rub with sea salt. Bake at 350 degrees for one hour, or until tender. Allow to cool 10 minutes. Meanwhile, cook bacon in a skillet over medium heat until crisp; drain, crumble and set aside. Slice potatoes lengthwise and scoop out insides into a bowl; set potato shells aside. Mash potato with bacon and remaining ingredients except green onions and Cheddar cheese; fold in half the green onions and half the Cheddar cheese. Evenly spoon mashed potato mixture back into potato shells; top with remaining cheese and green onions. Bake for 15 more minutes, or until cheese is melted and potatoes are heated through. Makes 8 servings.

Baked potatoes in a snap! Pierce 10 to 12 baking potatoes with a fork and wrap each in aluminum foil. Arrange potatoes in a slow cooker, cover and cook on high setting for 2-1/2 to 4 hours, until fork-tender.

SLAM-DUNK
Mains & Sides

Teriyaki Burgers

Connie McKone
Fort Atkinson, IA

These are so easy to make and a nice change from the average burger. My family loves them. The simple spiced mayonnaise adds a zip that just takes these burgers to a whole new level!

1/4 c. soy sauce
1/4 c. honey
2 cloves garlic, minced
1 t. ground ginger
1/3 c. mayonnaise

2 lbs. ground beef
1/8 t. salt
1/8 t. pepper
6 hamburger buns, split

In a large bowl, stir together soy sauce, honey, garlic and ginger. In a separate bowl, combine mayonnaise and 2 tablespoons soy sauce mixture; set aside. Add beef, salt and pepper to remaining soy sauce mixture. Mix well and shape into 6 patties. Grill patties over medium-high heat, turning once, until no longer pink in the center. Spread buns with mayonnaise mixture and top with a patty. Makes 6 burgers.

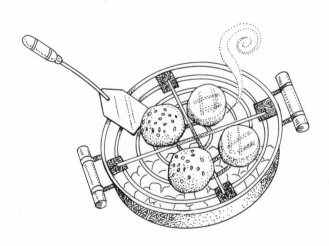

For the juiciest foods, flip grilled burgers with a spatula, and turn steaks, chicken and brats with tongs, not a fork. The holes a fork makes will let the juices escape.

Baked Sweet-and-Sour Chicken

Kristin Knowles
De Soto, IL

While the ingredients may look odd at first...don't fret. All these flavors come together to create one mouthwatering meal! Plus, this dish is healthier than take-out since nothing's fried.

16-oz. jar French salad dressing
10-oz. jar peach or apricot
  preserves
1-1/2 oz. pkg. onion soup mix
1 T. water
3 to 4 boneless, skinless chicken
  breasts, cubed

3 c. long-cooking rice, uncooked
15-1/4 oz. can pineapple chunks,
  drained
1 to 2 green peppers, chopped

In a lightly greased 13"x9" baking pan, combine salad dressing, preserves, soup mix and water. Stir in chicken until evenly coated. Bake, uncovered, at 350 degrees for 45 minutes, until chicken is no longer pink. Meanwhile, prepare rice according to package directions. Remove chicken from oven; stir in pineapple and green pepper. Bake for an additional 15 minutes. Serve over rice. Makes 8 to 10 servings.

Why not serve up Asian dishes at home with chopsticks?
Ask for a couple extra pairs to take home the next time you get
take-out. They're usually more than happy to give you a few.

SLAM-DUNK
Mains & Sides

Sesame Pork Ribs

Barb Rudyk
Alberta, Canada

*This is a great slow-cooker recipe. The ribs have a really tasty
Asian flavor, and the meat just falls right off the bone.*

3/4 c. brown sugar, packed
1/2 c. soy sauce
1/2 c. catsup
1/4 c. honey
2 T. vinegar
3 cloves garlic, pressed
1 t. salt

1 t. ginger
1/4 to 1/2 t. red pepper flakes
5 lbs. pork spareribs, cut into
   serving-size pieces
1 onion, sliced
Garnish: 2 T. sesame seed,
   2 T. sliced green onion

In a large bowl, mix together brown sugar, soy sauce, catsup, honey,
vinegar, garlic and seasonings. Add ribs to brown sugar mixture; turn to
coat well. Place onion in a slow cooker; top with ribs and sauce. Cover
and cook on low setting for 5 to 6 hours, until ribs are very tender.
Remove ribs to a serving platter; garnish with sesame seed and green
onion. Serves 6.

Hosting a barbecue will guarantee
a big turnout of friends &
neighbors! Load grills with
chicken, ribs, brats, burgers and
hot dogs, then ask guests to bring
a favorite side dish or dessert
to share. Add some yard games
and everyone's a winner!

Marvelous Meatball Subs

Emily Martin
Ontario, Canada

There's nothing like a hearty meatball sub. All that yummy sauce and gooey cheese...better grab some extra napkins! These meatballs would also be scrumptious served over your favorite pasta.

1 lb. lean ground beef
1/2 lb. ground Italian pork
   sausage
2 c. Italian-flavored dry bread
   crumbs
1/2 c. grated Parmesan cheese
3 eggs, beaten
4 cloves garlic, minced
1/4 c. fresh Italian parsley,
   chopped

1 T. fresh basil, minced
1/4 t. red pepper flakes
1/2 t. salt
1/2 t. pepper
1/4 c. olive oil
24-oz. jar marinara sauce
crusty sub rolls, split
Garnish: shredded mozzarella
   cheese

In a large bowl, combine beef, sausage, bread crumbs, cheese, eggs, garlic, herbs and seasonings. Mix until well combined; form into 2-inch balls. Heat oil in a large skillet over medium heat. Cook meatballs in oil until browned on all sides, about 15 minutes; do not cook through. Remove meatballs to paper towels to drain. Pour pasta sauce into a large saucepan over low heat; spoon in meatballs. Simmer for 40 to 50 minutes, until meatballs are cooked through. To serve, spoon meatballs with some sauce into sub rolls; sprinkle with mozzarella cheese. Serves 6 to 8.

For a new twist, substitute packaged stuffing mix for
bread crumbs in meatball or meatloaf recipes.

SLAM-DUNK
Mains & Sides

Friday Night Pizza

Jennifer Levy
Warners, NY

This pizza has become my family's Friday night tradition. I make the dough early in the afternoon, and by dinnertime it's ready to go. If you don't have bread flour, you can use all-purpose flour instead.

1 env. active dry yeast
1/2 t. sugar
1 c. warm water
1/2 t. salt
1 T. olive oil
2-1/2 to 3 c. bread flour, divided
1 T. cornmeal

1 to 2 15-oz. can pizza sauce
assorted pizza toppings, such as
 pepperoni, sliced black olives
 and mushrooms
8-oz. pkg. shredded pizza-blend
 cheese

In a large bowl, dissolve yeast and sugar in very warm water, 110 to 115 degrees. Let stand 5 minutes. Add salt, olive oil and one cup flour to yeast mixture; mix well. Add another 1-1/2 to 2 cups flour; stir together until dough forms. Transfer dough to a lightly floured surface. Knead dough for 10 minutes, or until smooth and elastic. Place dough in another bowl that has been lightly greased with olive oil. Cover with a tea towel and let rise until double in bulk, about 1-1/2 to 2 hours. Sprinkle a 17"x11" jelly-roll pan with cornmeal. Punch dough down and spread evenly onto pan, making sure to press dough into corners. Spread desired amount of pizza sauce evenly over dough; top with desired toppings and cheese. Bake at 450 degrees for 12 to 15 minutes, until cheese is melted and crust is golden. Cut into squares. Serves 8.

Make the guests cheer...use toppings to spell out
"Go Team" on a Friday Night Pizza.

Spanish Rice in a Snap

Tiffani Schulte
Wyandotte, MI

My son just loves the rice we get with our meals in Mexican restaurants, so I decided to come up with a homemade version. He likes this one even better, and it couldn't be easier!

1-1/2 c. long-cooking rice,
    uncooked
2-1/2 c. water
10-oz. can diced tomatoes with
    green chiles

2 t. butter
2 t. chicken bouillon granules
1 t. chili powder
Optional: 1/4 to 1/2 t. smoked
    paprika

Combine all ingredients in a large saucepan over medium-high heat; bring to a boil. Cover and reduce heat. Simmer until rice is cooked and liquid is absorbed, about 20 minutes. Makes 6 servings.

Super-Easy Mac & Cheese

Sue Logan
Burnsville, MN

One day, my son asked me if we could make mac & cheese this way. I decided we should give it a try, and it turned out perfect... so good and so easy!

16-oz. pkg. elbow macaroni,
    uncooked
3 10-3/4 oz. cans Cheddar
    cheese soup
2-1/2 c. milk

1-1/4 c. water
16-oz. pkg. pasteurized process
    cheese spread, cubed
1 sleeve round buttery crackers,
    crushed

Place uncooked macaroni in a lightly greased 13"x9" baking pan; set aside. In a bowl, combine soup, milk and water; whisk to blend. Pour soup mixture over macaroni; stir to mix well. Fold in cubed cheese spread. Bake, covered with aluminum foil, at 425 degrees for 40 minutes. Remove from oven and sprinkle with crushed crackers. Return to oven, uncovered, and bake for 5 minutes longer. Makes 6 to 8 servings.

SLAM-DUNK
Mains & Sides

Prosciutto Burgers

Denise Jones
Fountain, FL

This is a family favorite, and the prosciutto add a deliciously different flavor to the juicy burgers.

1 to 1-1/2 lbs. ground beef
1/2 c. dry bread crumbs
1 to 2 t. dried parsley
1 egg, beaten
2 T. milk
1/2 c. grated Parmesan cheese
1/4 c. sun-dried tomatoes,
    chopped

3/4 t. salt
3/4 t. pepper
6 slices prosciutto ham
1/4 c. olive oil
6 hamburger buns, split
6 slices tomato
Garnish: grated Parmesan cheese

In a large bowl, mix together beef, bread crumbs, parsley, egg, milk, cheese, sun-dried tomatoes, salt and pepper. Form mixture into 6 patties. Wrap each patty with a slice of prosciutto. Heat oil in a large skillet over medium heat. Fry patties in oil for 3 to 4 minutes per side, until prosciutto is crisp and burgers reach desired doneness. Serve each burger topped with a slice of tomato and sprinkled with Parmesan cheese. Makes 6 burgers.

Tuck burgers into the pockets of halved pita rounds...
easy for small hands to hold and a tasty change from
the same old hamburger buns.

Mitchell's Wonderful Brisket

Liz Plotnick-Snay
Gooseberry Patch

We don't eat a lot of red meat, but we treat our family & friends to my husband's amazing brisket on special occasions and get-togethers.

5-lb. beef brisket
salt and pepper to taste
1 t. garlic powder
1 onion, sliced
1 bay leaf
10 to 12 whole cloves

3/4 c. chili sauce
1 T. Worcestershire sauce
1/2 c. water
1/4 c. brown sugar, packed
1/2 t. paprika

Sprinkle all sides of brisket with salt, pepper and garlic powder. Place in an ungreased 13"x9" baking pan. Lay sliced onion and bay leaf on top of brisket. Cover and refrigerate for 2 to 3 hours. Bake brisket, covered, at 300 degrees for 3 hours. Remove from oven and evenly stick cloves into brisket. In a bowl, combine remaining ingredients. Stir to mix well; pour over brisket. Bake for one hour longer. Remove bay leaf and cloves; slice to serve. Serves 10 to 12.

Don't trim the fat from your brisket until after it's done cooking. Not only does the fat provide flavor, it also helps in keeping the brisket from drying out.

SLAM-DUNK
Mains & Sides

Texas Cowboy Beans

Sara Jane Inman
Pomona, MO

These beans are practically a meal in themselves! A big pan of cornbread and a tall glass of iced tea are all you need to make them into a quick & easy dinner.

1-1/2 lb. ground beef
8 slices bacon, chopped
1 onion, chopped
16-oz. can butter beans
15-oz. can pork and beans
16-oz. can pinto beans
16-oz. can kidney beans
1/4 c. catsup

2 t. mustard
1/4 c. barbecue sauce
2 T. light corn syrup
1/3 c. brown sugar, packed
1 t. chili powder
1 t. salt
1 t. pepper

Brown beef in a skillet over medium heat; drain. Combine beef, bacon, undrained beans and remaining ingredients in a lightly greased 13"x9" baking pan; stir to mix well. Bake, uncovered, at 350 degrees for 45 minutes. Let stand for 5 minutes to thicken before serving. Makes 10 to 12 servings.

Nothing goes better with hearty baked beans than warm cornbread! Bake it in a vintage cast-iron skillet...cornbread will bake up with a crisp golden crust.

Onside Kickin' Chicken Kabobs

Melody Taynor
Everett, WA

I made these for a tailgating party one time and they were a huge hit. Turns out that our team ended up winning the game with a recovered onside kick, so I just had to name this recipe in their honor!

2 T. olive oil
2 T. fresh cilantro, chopped
juice of one lime
1 t. ground cumin
salt and pepper to taste
2 boneless, skinless chicken
    breasts, cubed

1 zucchini, sliced
1 onion, cut into wedges
1 red pepper, cut into 1-inch
    pieces
10 cherry tomatoes

In a bowl, combine oil, cilantro, lime juice and seasonings. Add chicken; stir to mix well. Cover and refrigerate for at least one hour. Thread chicken, zucchini, onion, red pepper and tomatoes onto skewers. Grill skewers over high heat, turning occasionally, for about 10 minutes, or until chicken is no longer pink in the center. Makes 4.

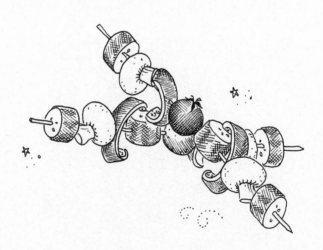

Soak wooden skewers in water for 30 minutes before
you grill so they don't burn.

SLAM-DUNK
Mains & Sides

Chicken Wings 4 Ways

Jocelyn Medina
Phoenixville, PA

So many sauces, so little time. Why not try a little of each?

2-1/2 lbs. chicken wings, thawed
   if frozen

Place wings in a 13"x9" baking pan. Bake wings, turning once, at 425 degrees for one hour; drain. For each sauce variation, combine all ingredients in a saucepan over medium-low heat. Cook and stir until combined. Toss wings in desired sauce. Serves 6 to 8.

Buffalo:

1/3 c. butter   1/2 c. hot pepper sauce

Tex-Mex:

1/3 c. butter   1/4 t. garlic powder
1 t. chili powder

Sweet & Spicy:

1/3 c. butter   3/4 t. cinnamon
1/4 c. orange juice

Asian:

1/3 c. butter   2 t. ground ginger
2 T. teriyaki sauce

Jane's Barbecue Wings

Brenda Saylor
Tiffin, OH

This recipe was shared by a family friend. My sons always insist on having wings on game day. These are quick, easy and yummy. Your family will be hooked once you try them.

1 c. brown sugar, packed
1 c. catsup
2-1/2 lbs. chicken wings,
  thawed if frozen

2 c. cola

In a bowl, mix together brown sugar and catsup; set aside. Place wings in an electric skillet on medium setting. Spoon brown sugar mixture evenly over wings; pour cola over all. Cook wings, uncovered, for 30 minutes, or until wings are cooked through and sauce is thickened. Serves 6 to 8.

Pittsburgh Pigskin Pierogies

Cyndy DeStefano
Mercer, PA

Football and Sundays mean good eating at our house! This dish is one of our favorites. It's quick to make and easy to eat while cheering on our favorite team.

2 T. butter
1 sweet onion, chopped
14-oz. Kielbasa sausage ring,
  sliced

16-oz. pkg. frozen potato &
  Cheddar cheese pierogies
1/2 t. garlic powder
salt and pepper to taste

Melt butter in a skillet over medium heat. Sauté onion until translucent. Add Kielbasa and pierogies to onion mixture; sprinkle with garlic powder, salt and pepper. Cook, stirring occasionally until pierogies and Kielbasa are golden and heated through. Serves 4.

SLAM-DUNK
Mains & Sides

Upper Peninsula Pasties

Bee Wilkening
Tarpon Springs, FL

This recipe was passed down from my grandmother who was born and raised in Wales, and now I'm a gramma passing the story on. Pasties originated with coal miners who took them into the mines since they are so easy to make and carry. Our families love them just because they are yummy cold weather food and super-simple.

2 9-inch pie crusts
5 potatoes, peeled and sliced
1 onion, chopped
1 lb. beef sirloin, cut into 1-1/2
　　inch strips

1/4 c. butter, sliced
salt and pepper to taste
Optional: 2 cloves garlic, minced

Separate and roll dough into 4 thin circles. Evenly arrange potatoes, onion and beef over half of each dough piece. Dot with butter and sprinkle with salt, pepper and garlic, if using. Fold dough over filling; pinch together seams to seal. Pierce tops of pasties with a fork to vent. Place pasties on an aluminum foil-lined baking sheet. Bake at 400 degrees for 45 minutes, or until golden and beef is fully cooked. Makes 4 servings.

The words "Play Ball!" mark the start of baseball season, so why not organize a neighborhood game? Make your own pennant, and join in the fun!

Smoky Stuffed Peppers

Anne McMaster
Portland, OR

These vegetarian stuffed peppers can be both a main dish and a perfect side to quesadillas or fajitas. Make them a little spicier by adding some cayenne pepper or a spoonful of hot salsa!

8 green peppers, tops removed
salt and pepper to taste
3 c. cooked rice
15-oz. can black beans, drained
   and rinsed
11-oz. can Mexican-style corn,
   drained
1 onion, chopped

1 c. chopped walnuts
4-oz. can chopped green chiles
1/2 t. smoke-flavored cooking
   sauce
1/2 t. ground cumin
1/2 c. shredded Monterey Jack
   cheese
Garnish: sliced jalapeño pepper

Bring a stockpot of water to a boil and boil peppers, a few at a time, for 5 minutes; drain. Season insides of peppers with salt and pepper; set aside. In a bowl, combine remaining ingredients except cheese and garnish; stir. Add additional salt and pepper to taste. Spoon one cup rice mixture into each pepper. Stand peppers in an ungreased 13"x9" baking pan. Bake, covered with aluminum foil, for 20 minutes. Remove foil and sprinkle peppers with cheese. Bake for an additional 5 to 10 minutes, until cheese is melted. Garnish with sliced jalapeño. Serves 8.

Smoky Stuffed Peppers will stand upright nicely when arranged in a Bundt® pan before baking.

SLAM-DUNK
Mains & Sides

Arroz con Pollo

Rosanna Catalano Flury
Tallahassee, FL

This is an old family recipe that I learned from my mom. Actually, this might be the first time it's been written down! It's easy to adjust the seasonings to your personal tastes. You'll find the sofrito, a tomato cooking base, and recaíto, a cilantro cooking base, in the international aisle of the grocery store.

1 c. olive oil
1 yellow onion, diced
2 lbs. boneless chicken thighs,
    cut into 1 to 2-inch pieces
5 cloves garlic, chopped
1/2 t. pepper
1/2 t. dried basil
1/2 t. dried oregano
1/8 t. chili powder

1/8 t. red pepper flakes
3 T. recaíto cooking base
3 T. sofrito cooking base
Optional: 1/2 to 3/4 c. beer
1 t. salt
8-oz. can tomato sauce
4 c. water
3 c. jasmine rice, uncooked

Heat oil in a large skillet over medium heat. Sauté onion until translucent. Add remaining ingredients except rice; bring to a boil. Cook and stir for 8 minutes, until chicken is nearly cooked through. Add rice to skillet. Cook, stirring constantly for 15 minutes, until most of the liquid is absorbed. Reduce heat to low and cover; simmer for 20 more minutes. Serves 6 to 8.

There are lots of different colors and flavors of sofrito,
from green to red and from mild to spicy. Try using it to
season beans, rice, stews or even hamburgers.

Tasty Fajitas

Joanna Cherry
Tampa, FL

My husband says that these fajitas are a keeper! The tasty marinade also works well for grilled chicken or pork chops.

1/4 c. lime juice
3 T. olive oil
1 t. garlic, minced
1 T. soy sauce
1 t. smoke-flavored cooking
   sauce
1 t. salt
1/4 t. pepper
1/2 t. ground cumin

1/4 t. Montreal steak seasoning
2 lbs. beef sirloin, pounded flat
   and sliced into 1-1/2 inch
   strips
1 green pepper, sliced
1 red pepper, sliced
3 green onions, sliced
1 doz. 10-inch flour tortillas

In a large plastic zipping bag, combine lime juice, oil, garlic, sauces and seasonings. Add beef to bag and refrigerate for 30 minutes to one hour. Place a large skillet over high heat. Place half of beef in skillet; sauté for about 4 minutes, until beef starts to brown. Add half the peppers and onions to skillet; cook until vegetables are crisp-tender and beef is cooked through. Remove to a bowl and repeat with remaining beef and vegetables; discard marinade. Spoon mixture into tortillas to serve. Serves 6 to 8.

Whether it's Fiesta Night, 1950s Diner or Hawaiian Luau, a theme suggests appropriate dishes, decorations and music. It gives guests something fun on their calendars to look forward to!

Enchilada Lasagna

Judi Lance
Payson, AZ

This is our family's favorite dish. The cream cheese is what really makes this dish wonderful. Pair with a crisp fresh salad, and dinner is served!

1 lb. lean ground beef
1 onion, chopped
1 green pepper, chopped
1 red pepper, chopped
8-oz. pkg. cream cheese, cubed
1 t. garlic powder

10-oz. can red enchilada sauce
6 8-inch corn tortillas
1 c. shredded Cheddar cheese, divided
Optional: sour cream, salsa

In a large skillet over medium heat, sauté beef, onion and peppers until beef is no longer pink. Drain; stir in cream cheese and garlic powder. Cook and stir until cheese is melted; remove from heat and set aside. Pour enchilada sauce into a shallow bowl. Dip 2 tortillas into sauce and place in a lightly greased 13"x9" baking pan. Spread tortillas with half the beef mixture; sprinkle with 1/3 cup shredded cheese. Repeat layers; top with remaining tortillas, sauce and cheese. Bake, uncovered, at 400 degrees for 20 to 25 minutes, until heated through and cheese is melted. Serve with sour cream and salsa, if desired. Serves 6.

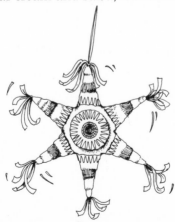

It's good sportsmanship not to pick up
lost golf balls while they are still rolling.

–Mark Twain

Buffalo Chicken Stromboli

Vickie

Here's a spicy, unique take on traditional stromboli.

2 c. cooked chicken, cubed
  or shredded
1/4 c. crumbled blue cheese

3 T. hot pepper sauce
17.3-oz. pkg. frozen puff pastry,
  thawed

In a large bowl, stir together chicken, cheese and hot sauce. Unfold one sheet puff pastry onto a lightly floured surface, reserving remaining sheet for another recipe. Roll out pastry to a 14-inch by 10-inch rectangle. Spoon chicken mixture down the center of the pastry. Fold long sides of pastry to the center over the filling; press edges to seal. Place seam-side down on an ungreased baking sheet; fold under ends. Bake at 400 degrees for 30 minutes, or until golden. Serves 4.

Turkey & Potato Hand Pies

Tori Willis
Champaign, IL

These little hand pies are perfect for parties or gatherings...no plates, no mess!

2 T. olive oil
1 onion, finely chopped
salt and pepper to taste
1 russet potato, peeled and diced
1 t. curry powder
3/4 c. peas

1/4 c. golden raisins, chopped
1 T. red wine vinegar
1-1/2 c. cooked turkey, shredded
2 9-inch pie crusts
1 egg, beaten

Heat oil in a large skillet over medium heat. Add onion, salt and pepper to oil. Cover and cook, stirring occasionally, for 4 minutes. Add potato to skillet and cook, covered, stirring occasionally until potato is tender, about 6 to 7 minutes. Stir in curry powder; remove from heat. Add peas, raisins and vinegar; mix to combine. Fold in turkey. Cut each pie crust into 4 triangles. Divide turkey mixture evenly among triangles. Fold dough over filling, pressing seams together with a fork to seal. Place hand pies on a baking sheet and brush with beaten egg. Bake at 400 degrees for 15 to 20 minutes, until golden. Serves 4.

SLAM-DUNK
Mains & Sides

Junkyard Joes

Natalie McKnight
Columbus, OH

I love this slow-cooker recipe...it's so quick & easy. I have made this since my kids were little. Now that they're grown, they are making it for their own kids!

3 to 4 lbs. ground beef
2 14-oz. pkgs. mini smoked
   sausages
1 lb. hot dogs, sliced into
   bite-size pieces
6-oz. pkg. sliced pepperoni
2 16-oz. cans Sloppy Joe sauce

10-3/4 oz. can tomato soup
1-1/4 c. water
Worcestershire sauce to taste
sandwich buns, split
8-oz. pkg. shredded Cheddar
   cheese

Brown beef in a large skillet over medium heat. Drain and spoon into a large slow cooker. Add smoked sausages, hot dogs and pepperoni slices to beef. Pour Sloppy Joe sauce, tomato soup, water and Worcestershire sauce into beef mixture. Stir to mix well. Cover and cook on low setting for 2 to 3 hours, until heated through. Spoon mixture onto buns; top with cheese. Serves 10 to 12.

Make it easy for guests to mingle and chat...set up food at several tables instead of one big party buffet. Place hot foods on one table, chilled foods at another, sweets at yet another.

Kim's Crustless Pizza

Kim Wallace
Dennison, OH

Tastes like a pizza, cuts like a pizza, yet there's no dough so you'll need a fork! This smells wonderful while it is baking, and if you have any leftovers, they taste just as good the next day...maybe even better! Everyone who tastes this says it is absolutely delicious!

2 lbs. lean ground beef
garlic salt, pepper and dried,
   minced onion to taste
2 c. shredded mozzarella cheese
16-oz. jar pizza sauce
1 c. shredded Italian-blend
   cheese

assorted pizza toppings, such as
   sliced pepperoni, onion, green
   pepper, banana pepper rings
   and mushrooms

Brown beef with seasonings in a skillet over medium heat; drain. In a bowl, stir together beef and mozzarella cheese. Spread beef mixture evenly in an ungreased 17"x11" jelly-roll pan. Top beef mixture with pizza sauce, Italian-blend cheese and pizza toppings. Bake at 350 degrees for 25 minutes, or until cheese is melted and golden. Let stand 5 minutes before slicing. Serves 8 to 10.

October is National Pizza Month so treat game-day fans to Kim's Crustless Pizza for dinner. Serve with plates, cutlery and napkins in your favorite team's colors.

SLAM-DUNK
Mains & Sides

Game-Day Garden Pizza

Paula Marchesi
Lenhartsville, PA

This pizza is so delicious, colorful and nutritious. I always serve it on game day to slip in something a little more healthy without them knowing. Sometimes I cut this pie into smaller pieces to make little appetizers.

1 loaf frozen bread dough,
   thawed
6 slices mozzarella cheese
8-oz. can pizza sauce
1 c. shredded Asiago cheese
1/2 c. broccoli flowerets, finely
   chopped
1/2 c. cauliflower flowerets,
   finely chopped

1/2 c. sliced mushrooms
1/4 c. red onion, finely chopped
1/4 c. green pepper, finely
   chopped
1/4 c. fresh spinach, finely
   chopped
1/2 c. cooked chicken, chopped
1 c. shredded mozzarella cheese

Roll dough out into a 15-inch round. Transfer dough to a lightly greased 14" round pizza pan; roll edge to form a crust. Place sliced mozzarella cheese over dough; spoon sauce over mozzarella. Sprinkle sauce with Asiago cheese; top with chopped vegetables and chicken. Sprinkle shredded mozzarella cheese over all. Bake at 425 degrees for 15 minutes, or until cheese is melted and crust is golden. Cut into wedges. Serves 4 to 6.

Keep all those garden-fresh veggies fresh longer. Most veggies should be kept in the refrigerator with the exception of potatoes, sweet potatoes, onions and eggplant. Tomatoes will keep their flavor best if stored on the counter, not in the refrigerator.

Karolina's Oven-Fried Chicken

Karol Cloutier
Alberta, Canada

I've been making this fried chicken since I was about seven...it's my mother's recipe. The breading on this chicken is so crunchy and golden, and the chicken unbelievably moist and tender.

1/2 c. all-purpose flour
2 T. curry powder
2 T. barbecue seasoning
2 T. Montreal steak seasoning
2 T. paprika
2 T. pepper

2 T. cayenne pepper
2 T. garlic powder
2 c. dry bread crumbs
2 eggs
2-1/2 lbs. chicken drumsticks

In a shallow bowl, combine flour and seasonings; set aside. Place bread crumbs in a separate shallow bowl; set aside. Whisk eggs in another bowl until well beaten. Working in batches, dredge drumsticks in flour mixture, then eggs, then bread crumbs. Place coated drumsticks on an aluminum foil-lined baking sheet. Bake chicken at 350 degrees for 45 minutes, or until golden and juices run clear when chicken is pierced with a fork. Makes 4 servings.

Keep color and texture contrasts in mind as you plan dinner.
For example, team crispy, golden-fried chicken with creamy
white macaroni salad and juicy red tomato slices...
everything will taste twice as good!

SLAM-DUNK
Mains & Sides

Tailgate Roast

Julie Ann Perkins
Anderson, IN

What a super sandwich for the football season...no one will turn these down. Pair with your favorite buns and watch the satisfied faces of all your fans light up!

4-lb. beef chuck roast
salt and pepper to taste
2 T. oil
12-oz. bottle chili sauce

1 T. Worcestershire sauce
1 onion, chopped
12-oz. can cola
sandwich buns, split

Season roast with salt and pepper. Heat oil in a skillet over medium-high heat. Sear roast on both sides in hot oil. Place roast in a large slow cooker. In a bowl, combine sauces, onion and cola; mix well. Pour sauce mixture over roast. Cover and cook on low setting for 8 to 9 hours, until roast is very tender. Shred roast with 2 forks; serve on buns. Serves 6 to 8.

Super Bowl Brisket

Susan Butterworth
Harper, TX

This is a game-day favorite no matter where I go. I usually end up making a bunch!

2 2 to 3-lb. center-cut beef
  briskets, trimmed

8-oz. bottle Italian salad dressing
Montreal steak seasoning to taste

Place briskets in a gallon-size plastic zipping bag; pour dressing over top. Marinate, refrigerated, for 24 hours. Remove briskets from bag and discard marinade. Season briskets with steak seasoning; wrap tightly in aluminum foil. Place briskets in an ungreased 13"x9" baking pan. Bake at 325 degrees for 3 hours. Reduce heat to 300 degrees and bake for another 1-1/2 to 2 hours. Let briskets stand, wrapped in foil, for about 15 minutes before serving. Slice to serve. Serves 8 to 10.

Nana's Baked Beans

Edna Cumbee Worth
Phenix City, AL

These are my famous baked beans I serve at every barbecue and lots of other occasions. My oldest daughter recently married...of course, my baked beans were served at the reception, much to everyone's delight!

1/2 lb. thick-sliced bacon, chopped
1 sweet onion, chopped
1 c. dark brown sugar, packed
1/3 c. molasses

1/4 c. Worcestershire sauce
1 T. mustard
3/4 c. catsup
2 15-oz. cans pork & beans, partially drained

In a deep skillet over medium heat, cook bacon until crisp; drain. Add remaining ingredients except pork & beans to bacon. Reduce heat to low; stir to mix. Add pork & beans to bacon mixture; mix well. Spoon bean mixture into a lightly greased 3-quart casserole dish. Bake, uncovered, at 350 degrees for about 30 minutes, until bubbly and heated through. Serves 8.

A western theme is fun and easy for casual get-togethers.
Set the table with pie plates, Mason jar tumblers and bandanna napkins. Serve up grilled burgers and fixin's, baked beans and tortilla chips with salsa.

SLAM-DUNK
Mains & Sides

Judi's Green Chile & Cheddar Bread

Judi Teasdale
Torrey, UT

This no-yeast, no-knead, no-rise quick bread is so easy and yummy. It goes well with some barbecued chicken and a big helping of coleslaw or baked beans.

3 c. self-rising flour
1/4 c. sugar
1/2 t. garlic powder
1-1/2 c. shredded Cheddar
   cheese, divided
4-oz. can diced green chiles

12-oz. can beer or non-alcoholic
   beer
Optional: 1 t. caraway seed
1/4 c. butter, melted
1/2 t. pico de gallo seasoning

In a large bowl, stir together flour, sugar, garlic powder, one cup cheese, chiles, beer and caraway seed, if using. Spoon batter into a lightly greased 9"x5" loaf pan. Drizzle melted butter over batter; sprinkle with remaining cheese and pico de gallo. Bake at 350 degrees for 50 to 60 minutes, until golden. Makes 12 servings.

No self-rising flour in the pantry? Try this! To equal one cup self-rising flour, substitute one cup all-purpose flour plus 1-1/2 teaspoons baking powder and 1/2 teaspoon salt.

Mexican Cornbread

Cheryl Givens
Dickson, TN

When I worked at a nursing home, we made this cornbread and I loved it. When I whipped up this recipe at home, my family fell in love with it too, especially my son. Now, he makes the cornbread, and it turns out even better than mine!

1-1/2 c. shredded sharp Cheddar
   cheese, divided
1-1/2 c. cornmeal
1 c. buttermilk
2 eggs, beaten

1 T. green pepper, chopped
1 c. creamed corn
1/2 t. red pepper flakes
1/2 c. oil

In a bowl, combine one cup cheese and remaining ingredients except oil; stir to mix well. Heat oil in a cast-iron skillet over medium heat. Pour batter into skillet; sprinkle remaining cheese over top. Transfer skillet to oven. Bake at 400 degrees for 40 to 45 minutes, until a toothpick inserted near the center tests clean. Makes 8 servings.

A fun new way to serve cornbread...mix up the batter, thin slightly with a little extra milk, then bake until crisp in a waffle iron.

SLAM-DUNK
Mains & Sides

Tostada Pizza

Kara Guilliams
Creve Coeur, IL

A Mexican twist on an Italian dish! Spice it up by adding some crushed red pepper flakes or fresh diced jalapeño pepper...make it even tastier by using queso fresco instead of Cheddar cheese.

1 lb. ground beef
1-1/4 oz. pkg. taco seasoning
  mix
1 t. chili powder
4-oz. can diced green chiles,
  drained
3/4 c. water
1 T. cornmeal
10-oz. tube refrigerated pizza
  dough

16-oz. can refried beans with
  chiles
8-oz. bottle taco sauce
1 c. shredded Cheddar cheese
1 c. shredded lettuce
1 tomato, chopped
1/2 c. green onions, sliced

Brown beef in a skillet over medium heat; drain. Add taco seasoning, chili powder, chiles and water to beef. Bring to a boil; reduce heat and simmer for 20 minutes, or until liquid is evaporated. Meanwhile, sprinkle cornmeal in a lightly greased 13"x9" baking pan. Roll pizza dough into a 12-inch by 8-inch rectangle; place in pan. Bake at 400 degrees for 5 minutes. Spread refried beans evenly over baked crust. Pour taco sauce over beans; spoon beef mixture over sauce. Bake for 10 minutes, until crust is golden. Sprinkle with cheese; bake for an additional 2 minutes, or until cheese is melted. Top with lettuce, tomato and onions before serving. Serves 6.

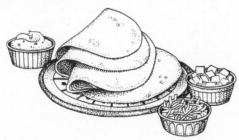

Fix a double batch! Brown two pounds of ground beef with two packages of taco seasoning mix, then freeze half of the mixture for a quick meal of tacos or taco salad another night.

Hot Dog Boats

Debra Manley
Bowling Green, OH

This was my Grandma Bright's recipe. She used to say, "You don't have to impress friends with fancy food, so keep it simple. If it looks good and tastes good, that will be impressive enough!" This recipe was, and still is, definitely a backyard favorite.

2 slices bacon, crisply cooked
    and crumbled
5-oz. jar pasteurized processed
    sharp cheese spread
1 T. green pepper, finely chopped

1 T. onion, finely chopped
8 hot dogs
8 hot dog buns, toasted
4 sweet pickle spears, halved
    lengthwise

In a bowl, combine bacon, cheese spread, green pepper and onion; mix well. Make a 3-inch lengthwise cut in each hot dog, without cutting all the way through. Fill each hot dog with about one tablespoon cheese mixture. Stand up a pickle spear in the middle of each hot dog to make a "sail." Grill hot dogs over medium heat until browned and cheese is bubbly. Place in buns to serve. Makes 8 servings.

Hot dog buns just taste better toasted...they won't get soggy either. Simply butter buns lightly and place on a hot grill for 30 seconds to one minute, until toasted to taste.

SLAM-DUNK
Mains & Sides

Jo Jo Potatoes

Shelly Turner
Boise, ID

*These crunchy potatoes are wonderful with fried chicken
or some crispy baked fish!*

1/2 c. all-purpose flour
3/4 t. lemon pepper
1/2 t. garlic powder
1/2 t. onion powder
1/4 t. celery salt

1/4 t. seasoned salt
4 potatoes, cut into 1/2-inch
   thick wedges
1 egg, beaten
oil for deep frying

In a shallow dish, mix together flour and seasonings. Dip potato wedges
in egg, then in flour mixture. Heat 2 inches of oil to 375 degrees in a
large saucepan. Working in batches, fry potatoes in oil until golden,
about 5 to 7 minutes. Drain on paper towels. Serves 4.

Fishing Buddies Hushpuppies

Nelda Columbo
Port Arthur, TX

*After a day spent on the lake, my uncle and his buddies always
made these to eat with the fish they caught.*

3 c. cornmeal
3 c. onions, chopped
1-1/2 c. all-purpose flour
3/4 c. sugar
3 T. baking powder
1 T. garlic salt

3 eggs, beaten
Optional: 2 jalapeño peppers,
   seeded and chopped
12-oz. can beer or non-alcoholic
   beer
oil for deep frying

In a bowl, combine all ingredients except oil; stir to mix well. Shape
batter into walnut-sized balls. Heat 2 inches of oil to 365 degrees in a
saucepan over medium-high heat. Fry hushpuppies, a few at a time, in
oil until golden. Drain on paper towels. Serves 10 to 12.

Tipsy Pork Chops

Harry Prior
Riverview, FL

I am 60 years old and have been married to the same wonderful woman for 41 years. We have 10 grandchildren! My wife works more than me, so I do most of the cookin'.

4 pork chops
12-oz. bottle beer or
   non-alcoholic beer

4 t. poultry seasoning
1/2 c. agave nectar, divided

Place pork chops in a large plastic zipping bag; pour beer over chops. Refrigerate for at least 8 hours. Remove chops from bag; discard marinade. Season both sides of chops with poultry seasoning. Place chops on a hot grill and brush tops with half the nectar. Cook for 7 minutes. Flip chops and brush with remaining nectar. Cook for another 7 minutes, or until chops are no longer pink in the center. Makes 4 servings.

Agave nectar is a liquid sweetener similar to honey. It's sweeter than sugar and made from the agave plant. It's normally found in stores near the honey.

3-Cheese Baked Spaghetti

Leah Beyer
Flat Rock, IN

I love to use ground pork in Italian dishes. I usually use cut spaghetti for baked spaghetti...bite-size pieces without all the hassle of breaking spaghetti.

7-oz. pkg. cut spaghetti,
   uncooked
1 lb. ground pork
1 egg, beaten
1 c. cottage cheese
2 c. shredded mozzarella cheese,
   divided

1 c. shredded Parmesan cheese,
   divided
28-oz. jar pasta sauce
1 t. Italian seasoning
1 t. garlic powder
1 t. salt
1/2 t. pepper

Cook spaghetti according to package directions; drain and set aside. Meanwhile, brown pork in a skillet over medium heat; drain. In a bowl, combine cooked spaghetti, egg, cottage cheese, one cup mozzarella cheese and 1/2 cup Parmesan cheese. Mix well. In a separate bowl, combine pork, spaghetti sauce and seasonings. Add spaghetti mixture to pork mixture; stir to combine. Spoon mixture into a lightly greased 13"x9" baking pan; sprinkle with remaining cheeses. Bake, uncovered, at 300 degrees for 30 minutes, or until bubbly and cheese is melted. Serves 6 to 8.

For baked casseroles with pasta, cook pasta for the shortest cooking time recommended on the package. It's not necessary to rinse the cooked pasta, just drain well.

Easy Stuffed Shells for a Crowd

Pat Martin
Riverside, CA

My husband and I love stuffed shells. One evening I decided to make them with what I had on hand to use up ingredients before going on vacation. What a delicious combination the fridge came up with!

1 lb. ground Italian pork sausage
1 lb. lean ground beef
1 t. garlic salt, divided
1 t. dried basil
1 t. dried thyme
2 32-oz. jars tomato-basil
  spaghetti sauce
12-oz. pkg. jumbo pasta shells,
  uncooked
1/2 t. pepper

2 t. dried parsley
1-1/2 c. low-fat ricotta cheese
8-oz. pkg. reduced-fat cream
  cheese, softened
1/2 c. crumbled lemon-garlic-
  oregano feta cheese
1 c. grated Parmesan cheese
Optional: 1 c. garlic croutons,
  crushed

Brown sausage and beef in a large stockpot over medium heat; drain. Season meat mixture with 1/2 teaspoon garlic salt, basil and thyme. Pour pasta sauce into stockpot; cover. Bring to a boil; reduce heat to low and simmer. Meanwhile, cook pasta shells according to package directions; drain and let cool slightly. In a bowl, combine remaining garlic salt, pepper, parsley and cheeses. Spread a layer of sauce mixture in 2 lightly greased 13"x9" baking pans. Fill each shell with about 2 tablespoons cheese mixture. Place each shell, cheese-side up, in baking pans; top with remaining sauce mixture. Sprinkle with crushed croutons, if using. Bake, uncovered, at 400 degrees for 30 to 35 minutes. Let stand 5 minutes before serving. Serves 12.

Cook and chill noodles for filled pasta dishes. It'll be so much easier to fill shells, and recipes will have one less step.

TOUCHDOWN
Treats

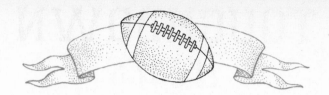

Derby Day Chocolate Pecan Pie

Marian Forck
Chamois, MO

I whip up this pie for our church picnics in Frankenstein, Missouri.
Make it even more authentic by adding just a splash of
Kentucky bourbon to the filling!

9-inch pie crust
6-oz. pkg. semi-sweet chocolate
   chips
1 c. chopped pecans
2 eggs, lightly beaten
1 t. vanilla extract

1/2 c. butter, melted and cooled
   slightly
1/2 c. brown sugar, packed
1/2 c. sugar
1/2 c. all-purpose flour

Line a 9" pie plate with pie crust; set aside. In a bowl, combine chocolate chips and remaining ingredients; mix well. Pour pie filling into crust. Bake at 325 degrees for one hour, or until center is set. Let cool completely before slicing. Serves 8.

Toting a pie to a picnic or party? A bamboo steamer
is just the thing...depending on its basket size, you may
even be able to take two pies at once.

TOUCHDOWN
Treats

Hoosier Cake

Sherry Sheehan
Phoenix, AZ

This recipe was handed down on my father's side of the family by my favorite aunt, Aunt Jeanette. She regularly brought this cake to family reunions, and it disappeared almost as quickly as it appeared.

1-1/2 c. hot water
1 c. quick-cooking oats,
   uncooked
1 c. light brown sugar, packed
1 c. sugar
1 t. vanilla extract
2 eggs

1/2 c. shortening
1-1/2 c. all-purpose flour
1 t. salt
1 t. baking soda
1 t. cinnamon
1 c. raisins

In a bowl, combine water and oats; set aside. In another bowl, combine sugars, vanilla, eggs and shortening. Mix well. Stir in oat mixture. Add remaining ingredients to oat mixture; stir to blend well. Spoon batter into a greased 13"x9" baking pan. Bake at 350 degrees for 35 to 40 minutes, until a toothpick inserted in the center tests clean. Remove from oven and cool; spread with Coconut-Pecan Frosting. Serves 12 to 15.

Coconut-Pecan Icing:

1/2 c. butter
1 c. brown sugar, packed
12-oz. can evaporated milk

1 t. vanilla extract
2 c. shredded coconut
1 c. chopped pecans

In a saucepan over medium heat, combine butter, brown sugar and milk. Bring to a boil and cook, stirring constantly, until thickened. Remove from heat; stir in vanilla, coconut and pecans.

For a toasty, nutty flavor, bake oats before they're used in recipes. Simply spread them on a baking sheet and bake for 10 to 12 minutes at 300 degrees...cool slightly before using.

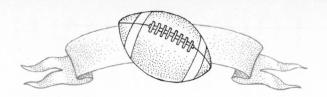

Spicy-Hot Brownies

Joshua Logan
Victoria, TX

These are unlike any other brownie I've ever had! The cayenne pepper adds a tasty kick that I just can't get enough of. Every person who tries one is at first surprised, but then they're coming back for seconds.

20-oz. pkg. chewy fudge
   brownie mix
1 t. chili powder
3/4 t. cayenne pepper
1/4 c. water
1 t. orange zest

4 t. frozen orange juice
   concentrate, divided
2 eggs, beaten
1/2 c. oil
16-oz. container cream cheese
   frosting

In a large bowl, stir together dry brownie mix and spices; set aside. In a cup, combine water, orange zest and one teaspoon orange juice concentrate. Add to brownie mix along with eggs and oil. Beat as package directs. Spread batter in a greased 8"x8" baking pan. Bake at 350 degrees for 42 to 45 minutes, until a toothpick inserted in center tests almost clean. Place pan on a wire rack; cool completely. Stir remaining orange juice concentrate into frosting; spread over cooled brownies. Cut into squares. Cover; keep refrigerated. Makes 16.

For perfectly cut brownies or bars, refrigerate them in the pan for about an hour after baking. Cut them with a plastic knife for a clean cut every time!

Minty Chocolate Brownies

Kristy Markners
Fort Mill, SC

*These brownies feature my five-year-old son's favorite cookie...
and any brownie that has crushed cookies as one of its
ingredients has got to be good!*

1/2 c. butter, melted
1 c. sugar
1 t. vanilla extract
2 eggs
1/2 c. all-purpose flour
1/3 c. baking cocoa

1/4 t. baking powder
1/4 t. salt
1/4 c. milk
7 chocolate-covered thin mint
  cookies, crushed

In a bowl, beat together butter, sugar and vanilla with an electric mixer on medium speed. Beat in eggs, one at a time, until fully combined. In a separate bowl, stir together flour, cocoa, baking powder and salt. Slowly add flour mixture to butter mixture, beating until well blended. Beat in milk. Fold in crushed cookies. Spread batter evenly in a lightly greased 9"x9" baking pan. Bake at 350 degrees for 35 to 40 minutes, until a toothpick inserted near the center tests clean. Cool completely in pan on a wire rack. Cut into squares. Makes one dozen.

Use a food processor or blender to quickly crush cookies. If you don't have one handy, place cookies in a large plastic zipping bag and crush them with a rolling pin.

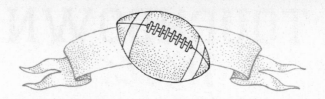

No-Bake Apple Pie

Deanna Polito-Laughinghouse
Knightdale, NC

The first time I saw this recipe in a very old magazine, I thought it sounded interesting. So I tried it, and it turned out to be one of the best apple pies I ever had! The best part? No oven is required...so it's perfect for summer cooking!

5 apples, peeled, cored and
   thinly sliced
1-3/4 c. water, divided
3-oz. pkg. lemon gelatin mix
1/2 t. cinnamon

1/4 t. nutmeg
3-oz. pkg. cook & serve vanilla
   pudding mix
1/2 c. chopped walnuts
9-inch graham cracker crust

In a large saucepan over medium heat, combine apples, 1-1/2 cups water, dry gelatin mix and spices. Bring to a boil. Reduce heat to low; cover. Simmer for 4 to 6 minutes, until apples are tender. Stir in dry pudding mix and remaining water. Cook and stir for 2 minutes, or until thickened. Remove from heat; fold in nuts. Spoon filling into crust; refrigerate overnight. Serves 8 to 10.

Try a savory topping on your next apple pie...a slice of sharp Cheddar cheese! The tangy saltiness of the cheese really brings out the sweet, cinnamon-y goodness of the apples.

TOUCHDOWN
Treats

Old-Fashioned Caramel Corn

Lisa Boyer
Stockbridge, MI

A friend gave me this recipe, and I've been making it for years. It's perfect for tailgating, Halloween, on a warm summer evening while watching movies, or just anytime you need a sweet treat.

6 qts. popped popcorn
2 c. brown sugar, packed
1/2 c. light corn syrup
1 c. butter

1/4 t. cream of tartar
1/8 t. salt
1/2 t. baking soda

Place popcorn in a large heat-proof bowl; set aside. In a large saucepan over medium heat, combine brown sugar, syrup, butter, cream of tartar and salt. Bring to a boil; cook for 5 minutes, stirring occasionally. Remove from heat; add baking soda and mix well. Pour caramel over popcorn; mix well with 2 wooden spoons. Spread caramel corn onto 2 parchment paper-lined baking sheets. Bake at 200 degrees for one hour. Break into pieces to serve. Makes 10 to 12 servings.

Ooey-Gooey Popcorn

Denise Webb
Savannah, GA

Okay....this is sticky and not diet food, but what a yummy treat to enjoy every once in awhile! This recipe was shared with me many, many years ago.

3 qts. popped popcorn
1/4 c. margarine

1/4 c. brown sugar, packed
2 c. mini marshmallows

Place popcorn in a large heat-proof bowl; set aside. In a saucepan over medium heat, combine butter, brown sugar and marshmallows. Cook, stirring constantly, until marshmallows are melted and mixture is smooth. Pour butter mixture over popcorn; toss to coat. Makes 4 servings.

Goofer Balls

Terri Scungio
Williamsburg, VA

My mother got this recipe from a dear friend many years ago and we never really knew how it got its name. They were one of my favorite cookies growing up, and now they're my daughter's favorite!

16-oz. pkg. powdered sugar
2-1/2 c. graham cracker crumbs
7-oz. pkg. sweetened flaked
   coconut
1 c. butter, melted

12-oz. jar crunchy peanut butter
12-oz. pkg. semi-sweet chocolate
   chips
1/2 bar paraffin wax

In a bowl, mix together sugar, cracker crumbs, coconut and butter. Stir in peanut butter. Roll into one-inch balls. Place balls on a baking sheet and chill. Meanwhile, melt chocolate chips and paraffin in a double boiler. Once chocolate mixture is melted and smooth, dip balls in chocolate mixture to coat. Let stand on baking sheets until chocolate is set. Makes about 2 dozen.

Serve up Goofer Ball kabobs...fun for a dessert buffet.
On wooden skewers, alternate cookie balls with bite-size fresh
or candied fruit pieces. Stand skewers in a vase or insert them
in a large foam ball.

TOUCHDOWN
Treats

Cocoa Snickerdoodles

Barbara Humiston
Tampa, FL

I love chocolate, and these snickerdoodles are just the best...
far better than the regular kind. My family loves them.
They go so well with an icy glass of milk for dunking!

1-1/2 c. sugar
1/2 c. butter, softened
1 t. vanilla extract
2 eggs
2-1/4 c. all-purpose flour
1/2 c. baking cocoa

1 t. cream of tartar
1/2 t. baking soda
1/4 t. salt
2 T. sugar
2 t. cinnamon

In a large bowl, beat together sugar and butter with an electric mixer on medium speed until light and fluffy. Beat in vanilla and eggs. In a separate bowl, combine flour, cocoa, cream of tartar, baking soda and salt. Beat flour mixture into butter mixture until well blended. In another bowl, combine sugar and cinnamon. Roll dough into one-inch balls; roll in cinnamon-sugar. Place dough balls 2 inches apart on ungreased baking sheets. Bake at 400 degrees for 6 to 9 minutes. Cool completely on wire racks. Makes about 4 dozen.

The high school grandstand is always full for the Friday night football game, so cheer on your team! Pack a basket of goodies to enjoy while the marching band performs at halftime... Cocoa Snickerdoodles and a thermos filled with warm cider would be just right.

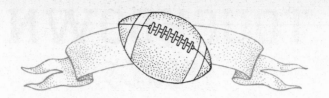

Devil's Food Cake

Nancy Grady Wilson
Kenansville, NC

This cake is unbelievably rich and moist. The frosting is tasty too, plus, it's scrumptious on other types of cakes.

1 c. brown sugar, packed
1 c. sugar
1 c. butter, softened
3 eggs, beaten
1/2 c. baking cocoa

1/2 c. buttermilk
2 c. self-rising flour
2 t. vanilla extract
1 t. baking soda
1 c. boiling water

In a large bowl, stir together all ingredients except baking soda and water; mix well. Dissolve baking soda in water; stir into brown sugar mixture. Evenly divide batter among 3 greased 8" round cake pans. Bake at 300 degrees for about 40 minutes, until toothpicks inserted in the centers test clean. Remove cakes from pans; cool. Frost with 7-Minute Frosting between layers and around outside of cake. Serves 18 to 20.

7-Minute Frosting:

3 egg whites
1 c. sugar
1/2 c. light corn syrup

3 T. cold water
1/2 t. cream of tartar
1 t. vanilla extract

Combine all ingredients in a double boiler over medium heat. Cook for 7 minutes, beating constantly with an electric mixer on medium speed until thickened.

Some say that Devil's Food Cake got its name from the reddish-brown color and, since it had such rich and delicious flavor, the taste was so good it was sinful!

TOUCHDOWN
Treats

Chipotle Caramels

Sharon Demers
Dolores, CO

My husband and I love caramels, and we also love a little spice. We decided to adapt this caramel recipe by adding a dash of chipotle chili powder. Now they have some kick!

1 c. butter
16-oz. pkg. brown sugar
1 c. light corn syrup
2 t. chipotle chili powder

1/8 t. salt
14-oz. can sweetened condensed
    milk
1 t. vanilla extract

Melt butter in a saucepan over medium heat. Add brown sugar, corn syrup, chili powder and salt; mix well. Slowly pour in condensed milk, stirring constantly. Cook and stir until mixture reaches the firm-ball stage, or 244 to 249 degrees on a candy thermometer. Remove from heat; stir in vanilla extract. Pour mixture into a greased 9"x9" baking pan. Cool completely; cut into squares. Wrap individual squares in wax paper if not serving immediately. Makes about 2-1/2 pounds.

For a nifty apple-shaped gift bag, fill red paper bags halfway with Chipotle Caramels. Trim a few inches off of the top then gather and secure it with a rubber band. Hide the rubber band and remaining paper top with green florists' tape to look like a stem.

Caramel Bananas

Betty Maxwell
Perrysburg, OH

I almost always have the ingredients on hand to make this recipe.
Be sure to use real vanilla, not imitation, and butter, not margarine.
It really makes a difference.

1-1/2 c. brown sugar, packed
1 c. cold water
1/4 c. all-purpose flour
3/4 c. milk

1/4 c. butter
1 T. vanilla extract
5 to 6 bananas, sliced lengthwise
3/4 c. chopped walnuts

Combine brown sugar and water in a saucepan over medium heat; bring
to a boil. Meanwhile, whisk together flour and milk in a bowl. Pour flour
mixture into sugar mixture. Boil for 2 to 3 minutes, until thickened;
remove from heat. Stir in butter and vanilla; cool completely. Arrange
sliced bananas on a serving plate. Spoon cooled caramel sauce over
sliced bananas; sprinkle with nuts. Makes 8 to 10 servings.

Banana Pudding Fudge

Leea Mercer
League City, TX

If you like banana pudding, you will love this! It's banana
pudding you can eat with your hands.

20 vanilla wafers, divided
14-oz. can sweetened condensed
  milk

2 T. butter
2-2/3 c. white chocolate chips
1 t. banana flavoring

Line an 8"x8" baking pan with parchment paper; lightly spray with
non-stick vegetable spray. Crush 8 vanilla wafers and sprinkle into pan;
set aside. In a saucepan over low heat, combine condensed milk, butter
and chocolate chips. Cook, stirring constantly, until chips are melted.
Remove from heat; stir in flavoring. Pour over crushed cookies in pan.
Top with remaining whole cookies. Cover and refrigerate for at least one
hour. Cut into squares to serve. Makes 3 dozen.

TOUCHDOWN
Treats

Peanut Butter Fudge Pie

Paula Christensen
Tooele, UT

This recipe was given to me by one of my husband's co-workers about 17 years ago. I made it one Thanksgiving, and my sisters have made sure that I've brought it every year since.

1-1/2 c. cream cheese, softened
1-1/2 c. creamy peanut butter
2 T. butter, softened
3 c. powdered sugar

1-1/2 T. vanilla extract
1-1/2 c. whipping cream, divided
2 9-inch graham cracker crusts
3/4 c. semi-sweet chocolate chips

In a bowl, beat cream cheese, peanut butter and butter with an electric mixer on medium speed until smooth. Stir in sugar and vanilla; set aside. In a separate bowl, beat 3/4 cup whipping cream with an electric mixer on high speed until stiff peaks form. Fold whipped cream into cream cheese mixture. Evenly divide filling between crusts; chill for 2 hours. Combine remaining whipping cream and chocolate chips in a saucepan over low heat. Cook, stirring constantly, until chips melt. Remove from heat; let cool slightly. Pour evenly over pies. Refrigerate again until set, about one hour. Makes 2 pies, each serves 8.

It's easy to make your own graham cracker crust. Mix 1-1/2 cups fine graham cracker crumbs, 1/4 cup sugar and 1/2 cup melted butter; press into a pie plate. Chill for 20 minutes or bake at 350 degrees for 10 minutes.

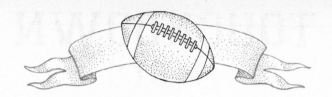

All-Star Boston Cream Pie

Flo Burtnett
Gage, OK

A classic pie that looks just as good as it tastes. Who can resist layers of cake, cream and rich chocolate?

5 eggs, separated
1 c. sugar, divided
1-1/2 t. lemon zest
4-1/2 t. lemon juice
2 T. water
1 c. cake flour
1/4 t. salt
1/4 t. cream of tartar
3.4-oz. pkg. cook & serve vanilla
   pudding mix

1-1/2 c. milk
1/2 c. whipping cream
1/8 t. vanilla extract
2 T. margarine
2 1-oz. sqs. unsweetened baking
   chocolate
1 to 1-1/2 c. powdered sugar

In a large bowl, beat together egg yolks and 1/2 cup sugar. In a separate bowl, whisk together zest, juice and water. Gradually beat zest mixture into yolk mixture until fluffy. Fold in flour until completely blended. In a separate bowl, beat egg whites, salt and cream of tartar with an electric mixer on high speed until stiff peaks form. Beat remaining sugar into egg whites until combined. Gently fold egg white mixture into yolk mixture until fully combined. Divide batter between 2 lightly greased 9"x9" round cake pans. Bake at 350 degrees for 25 minutes, or until a toothpick inserted near the center tests clean. Cool completely on wire racks. Meanwhile, prepare pudding mix according to package directions, using milk. Refrigerate until well chilled; fold in cream and vanilla. Set aside. Melt margarine and chocolate in a double boiler. Remove from heat; whisk in powdered sugar until smooth. To assemble, place one cake on a plate; spread with pudding mixture. Top pudding mixture with remaining cake; pour chocolate mixture over top. Serves 12 to 15.

When you deliver a pie to someone,
include the recipe...they'll be sure
to thank you!

TOUCHDOWN
Treats

Key Lime Pound Cake

Gina McClenning
Miami, FL

What do you do with a bagful of sweet little juicy Key limes from the farmers' market? Why, whip up some Key lime pound cake, of course!

1/2 c. butter, softened
1/2 c. shortening
3 c. sugar
6 eggs, separated
3 c. cake flour
1/4 t. baking powder

1/4 t. baking soda
1 c. sour cream
2 T. Key lime zest
1/2 c. Key lime juice
Garnish: powdered sugar, twists
    of lime zest, fresh raspberries

In a large bowl, beat together butter and shortening with an electric mixer on medium speed until fluffy. Gradually beat in sugar. Beat in egg yolks, one at a time, until well mixed. In a separate bowl, sift together flour, baking powder and baking soda. Gradually beat flour mixture into butter mixture, alternating with sour cream and ending with flour mixture. Beat in lime zest and lime juice. In another bowl, beat egg whites at high speed until stiff peaks form; fold into batter. Spoon batter into a lightly greased Bundt® pan. Bake at 325 degrees for 30 minutes, or until a toothpick inserted near the center tests clean. Remove cake from pan; cool completely on a wire rack. Dust with powdered sugar; garnish with twists of lime zest and raspberries. Serves 10 to 12.

Freshly grated citrus zest adds so much flavor to recipes,
and it's easy to keep on hand. Whenever you use an orange,
lemon or lime, just grate the peel first. Keep it frozen in
an airtight container for up to 2 months.

Margarita Watermelon Slices

Anne Alesauskas
Minocqua, WI

I made this one year as an adults-only treat, and it tasted just like a watermelon margarita...plus it's way more fun to eat!

1 seedless watermelon, sliced 1-inch thick and cut into quarters	3/4 c. water
	1 c. tequila
	3/4 c. Triple Sec
1 c. sugar	Garnish: lime wedges, coarse salt

Arrange watermelon slices in a single layer in two 13"x9" baking pans; set aside. In a saucepan over medium heat, combine sugar, water, tequila and Triple Sec. Bring to a boil. Cook, stirring occasionally, until sugar dissolves, about one minute. Remove from heat; let cool completely. Pour syrup over watermelon slices, turning to coat. Refrigerate for 45 minutes. Before serving, squeeze a lime wedge over watermelon slice; sprinkle with salt. Makes 12 to 14 servings.

Frozen Pineapple Slush

Judith Lalli
Roslyn, PA

This is a recipe my grandmother enjoyed at a church function many, many years ago. It is now a family favorite on hot summer days.

3 c. water	4 c. orange juice
2 c. sugar	15-1/4 oz. can crushed pineapple
4 c. lemonade	4 ripe bananas, mashed

In a saucepan over medium heat, combine water and sugar. Bring to a boil; stir until sugar is dissolved. Remove from heat and stir in remaining ingredients. Divide mixture between two 13"x9" baking pans. Freeze until solid. Remove pans from freezer a few minutes before serving to allow slush to soften. Scoop into bowls or cups to serve. Makes about 24 servings.

TOUCHDOWN *Treats*

Strawberry-Lemon Shortbread Bars

Coleen Lambert
Luxemburg, WI

The tartness of the lemon goes hand-in-hand with the sweetness of the strawberry preserves. These are sure to be one of the first desserts gone at your next game-day get-together or potluck.

2 c. all-purpose flour
1/2 c. powdered sugar
3/4 t. lemon zest, divided
3/4 c. chilled butter
2 8-oz. pkgs. cream cheese,
    softened

3/4 c. sugar
2 eggs
1 T. lemon juice
1 c. strawberry preserves

In a bowl, stir together flour, powdered sugar and 1/2 teaspoon lemon zest. Cut in butter with 2 forks until coarse crumbs form. Press flour mixture into an ungreased 13"x9" baking pan. Bake at 350 degrees for 20 to 25 minutes, until lightly golden. Cool completely. Meanwhile, beat together cream cheese and sugar with an electric mixer on medium speed until smooth. Add eggs, one at a time, beating until just blended. Beat in lemon juice and remaining zest. Spread preserves over cooled crust. Spread cream cheese mixture over preserves, spreading to edges of pan. Bake at 350 degrees for 25 to 30 minutes, until set. Cool for one hour on a wire rack. Cover and chill for 4 to 8 hours. Slice into bars to serve. Makes 14 to 16 bars.

Jams and preserves keep well, so pick up a few jars of local specialties like strawberry, peach or boysenberry. You'll be well stocked to bake up jam bars, linzer cookies or thumbprints!

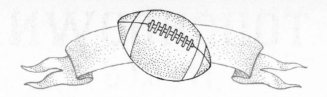

Apple Pie Cake

Becky Kirchoff
Omaha, NE

This mouthwatering recipe has been in my family for years.

1-1/4 c. sugar, divided
1/2 c. plus 2 T. butter, divided
1 egg
1 c. all-purpose flour
1 t. baking soda
1/4 t. nutmeg
1/4 t. cinnamon
2 c. apples, peeled, cored and
  diced

1/4 c. chopped nuts
1/2 c. brown sugar, packed
2 T. cornstarch
3/4 c. water
1 t. vanilla extract
1 t. salt

In a bowl, beat together one cup sugar, 1/2 cup butter and egg with an electric mixer on medium speed. Stir in flour, baking soda, spices, apples and nuts. Spoon batter into a lightly greased 8"x8" baking pan. Bake at 350 degrees for 30 minutes. Reduce heat to 325 degrees; bake an additional 20 minutes. Meanwhile, combine remaining sugar, remaining butter, brown sugar, cornstarch, water, vanilla and salt in a saucepan over medium heat. Bring to a boil; cook, stirring occasionally, until thickened. Drizzle sauce over warm cake. Serves 9.

Lemonade Pie

Beverley Williams
San Antonio, TX

You can substitute frozen limeade, orange juice concentrate or even frozen margarita mix for the lemonade.

14-oz. can sweetened condensed
  milk
12-oz. can frozen lemonade
  concentrate, thawed

8-oz. container frozen whipped
  topping, thawed
2 9-inch graham cracker crusts

In a bowl, mix together condensed milk, lemonade and whipped topping; evenly divide between crusts. Freeze overnight. Makes 2 pies; each serves 6 to 8.

TOUCHDOWN
Treats

77 Carrot Cake

Cristina West
Oklahoma City, OK

My husband loves carrot cake, so I made this for him. I named this recipe 77 Carrot Cake because the diamond on my wedding ring is .77 carat. I just love my wedding ring...it means so much to me. This one's for my hubby!

1/2 c. sugar
1/2 c. brown sugar, packed
1 c. applesauce
4 eggs, beaten
2 t. vanilla extract
2 c. all-purpose flour
2 t. baking soda

2 t. baking powder
1/2 t. salt
2 t. cinnamon
1/2 t. nutmeg
3 c. carrots, peeled and shredded
Garnish: additional shredded
   carrot

In a bowl, beat together sugars, applesauce, eggs and vanilla with an electric mixer on medium speed. Stir in flour, baking soda, baking powder, salt, cinnamon and nutmeg. Beat until well combined. Fold in carrots. Spoon batter into a lightly greased 13"x9" baking pan. Bake at 350 degrees for 25 to 30 minutes, until a toothpick inserted in the center tests clean. Cool in pan for 10 minutes. Remove from pan; cool completely on a wire rack. Spread Cream Cheese Frosting over cooled cake; garnish with shredded carrot. Keep refrigerated. Makes 24 servings.

Cream Cheese Frosting:

8-oz. pkg. cream cheese,
   softened
1/4 c. butter, softened

1 t. vanilla extract
2 c. powdered sugar

Combine all ingredients in a bowl. Beat with an electric mixer on medium speed until creamy.

Need a cake stand for your special creation? Set a plate
on an inverted bowl.

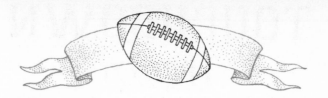

Citrus Soda Cake

Emily Phelps
Harrodsburg, KY

This recipe was given to me by my best friend's mother, Marsha, who was also my kindergarten teacher. Every time I make this cake, everyone wants the recipe, so be ready to share!

18-1/2 oz. pkg. yellow cake mix
3.4-oz. pkg. instant vanilla
  pudding mix
4 eggs, beaten
1/2 c. water

1/2 c. oil
3/4 c. citrus-flavored soda,
  divided
1/2 c. margarine
1 c. sugar

In a bowl, combine dry mixes, eggs, water, oil and 1/2 cup soda. Beat with an electric mixer on medium speed until well blended, about 2 minutes. Pour batter into a lightly greased Bundt® pan. Bake at 350 degrees for 55 minutes, or until a toothpick inserted into the cake tests clean. While still warm, poke holes in cake with with a fork; set aside. Melt margarine in a saucepan over low heat; add sugar and remaining soda. Boil for 2 minutes, or until thickened. Pour glaze over cake; let cool. Invert cake onto a serving plate. Serves 10 to 12.

Add some retro charm the next time you bake a Bundt® cake.
When serving, fill a vintage milk bottle with water and use it
to hold seasonal flowers in the center of the cake.

TOUCHDOWN
Treats

Marshmallow Treats-on-a-Stick

Martha Stapler
Sanford, FL

I was trying to make a different twist on marshmallow treats, and these were an instant hit!

14-oz. pkg. caramels, unwrapped
14-oz. can sweetened condensed
  milk
13-1/2 oz. pkg. crispy rice cereal
24 marshmallows
wooden skewers or fondue forks

Combine caramels and condensed milk in a saucepan over low heat. Cook, stirring occasionally, until caramels are melted. Remove from heat. Pour cereal into a large bowl. Place each marshmallow on a wooden skewer or fondue fork. Dip marshmallow in caramel; roll in cereal. Place coated marshmallows on parchment paper to cool. Makes 2 dozen.

S'mores Bars

Kim Freeman
West Mansfield, OH

I take these yummy bars to every cookout because they are so easy to tote along. The best part is, they need to be made the day ahead, so no last-minute prep!

3/4 c. butter, melted
1/4 c. sugar
2 sleeves graham crackers, finely
  crushed
3 c. milk chocolate chips
4 c. mini marshmallows

In a bowl, combine butter, sugar and crushed crackers. Reserve 1/4 cup for topping. Press remaining mixture into a greased 13"x9" baking pan. Bake at 350 degrees for about 12 minutes, until dry. Meanwhile, place chocolate chips in a microwave-safe bowl. Microwave on high setting for one to 2 minutes, stirring once, until melted. Spread melted chocolate over graham cracker crust. Top chocolate with mini marshmallows; sprinkle with reserved cracker crumb mixture. Broil until marshmallows are melted and top is golden. Let stand overnight; cut into bars. Makes 14 to 16.

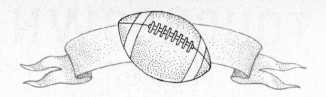

Pig-Out Cookies

Haley Carroll
Billings, MT

These cookies are decadent and truly delicious! Is there anything better than the combination of chocolate, peanut butter and bacon? Pour yourself a glass of milk and enjoy a seriously good cookie!

5 slices bacon
1-1/4 c. all-purpose flour
1/4 t. baking soda
1/4 t. baking powder
1/8 t. cinnamon
1/8 t. chili powder
1/4 t. salt

1/4 c. butter, softened
1/2 c. creamy peanut butter
1/2 c. sugar
1/2 c. brown sugar, packed
1 egg
1 t. vanilla extract
1/3 c. semi-sweet chocolate chips

Cook bacon until crisp in a skillet over medium heat. Crumble and drain, reserving 2 tablespoons drippings; set aside. In a large bowl, combine flour, baking soda, baking powder, cinnamon, chili powder and salt; set aside. In a separate bowl, beat together butter and reserved drippings with an electric mixer on medium speed until smooth. Beat in peanut butter and sugars until creamy, about 4 minutes. Add egg and vanilla; beat until fluffy, about 2 minutes. Reduce mixer setting to low; slowly beat in flour mixture until just combined. Fold in chocolate chips and bacon. Roll dough into 12 balls; arrange 2 inches apart on a parchment paper-lined baking sheet. Flatten balls slightly. Bake at 350 degrees for 12 to 14 minutes, until golden. Cool cookies on sheet for about 2 minutes; transfer to wire racks to cool completely. Makes one dozen.

If you're pressed for time, mix up cookie dough, pop it in the refrigerator, and bake later when guests arrive. They'll love walking in to the aroma of fresh-baked cookies!

TOUCHDOWN
Treats

Judy's Salty-Sweet Peanut Cookies

*Judy Borecky
Escondido, CA*

While my husband and three sons were watching the Chicago Bears, they would munch on sweet & salty glazed peanuts. I tossed some into my cookie batter one day, and voilà, this tasty recipe was born!

1 c. butter, softened
1-1/2 c. brown sugar, packed
2 eggs
1 t. vanilla extract
1-1/2 c. all-purpose flour

1 t. baking soda
1/2 t. salt
3 c. quick-cooking oats, uncooked
2 c. sweet & salty glazed peanuts

In a bowl, beat together butter and sugar with an electric mixer on medium speed until fluffy. Beat in eggs, one at a time, and vanilla until incorporated. In a separate bowl, stir together flour, baking soda and salt. Slowly beat flour mixture into butter mixture. Fold in oats and peanuts. Roll dough into one-inch balls and place on lightly greased baking sheets. Bake at 375 degrees for 12 minutes, or until golden. Makes about 4 dozen.

Toss together a yummy snack mix in a jiffy! Mix equal amounts of sweetened dried cranberries, salted peanuts and chocolate chips... great for munching on a game night or at get-togethers.

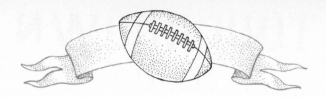

Malted Milk Squares

Mel Chencharick
Julian, PA

These squares taste just like a chocolate malt from your favorite soda fountain. I found this dessert in some recipes that belonged to my grandmother. She was truly the world's best grandma...a great cook and a great person.

1 c. graham cracker crumbs
2 T. sugar
2 T. butter, melted
2 eggs, separated
1 c. milk
1/4-oz. env. unflavored gelatin
1/3 c. dark brown sugar, packed

3 T. baking cocoa
1 t. vanilla extract
1 c. whipping cream
2 c. malted milk balls, coarsely
  crushed and divided
Garnish: whipped cream

In a bowl, mix together cracker crumbs, sugar and butter. Press into a lightly greased 9"x9" baking pan. Bake at 350 degrees for 10 minutes; cool completely. Meanwhile, whisk together egg yolks and milk in a saucepan. Stir in gelatin, brown sugar and cocoa; let stand one minute. Cook and stir over low heat for about 5 minutes, until gelatin is dissolved. Remove from heat; stir in vanilla. Pour mixture into a bowl and chill, stirring occasionally, until mixture begins to set. In a separate bowl, beat egg whites with an electric mixer on high speed until stiff peaks form. Fold egg whites into gelatin mixture. In a bowl, beat cream with an electric mixer on medium speed until stiff peaks form. Fold whipped cream and one cup crushed candy into gelatin mixture; spread evenly over crust. Chill until set; garnish with whipped cream and remaining crushed candy. Serves 9.

Going tailgating? Pack a scout-style pocketknife with can opener, corkscrew and other utensils in your picnic kit...so handy!

TOUCHDOWN
Treats

Jake's Magic Square Bars

Janet Morden
Ontario, Canada

This is my son's favorite dessert. He would ask me to bake these for him every time he came home from school. I taught him how to make them, and now he bakes them for his friends!

1 c. graham cracker crumbs
3 T. sugar
1/2 c. butter, melted
12-oz. pkg. semi-sweet chocolate
   chips
14-oz. can sweetened condensed
   milk
7-oz. pkg. sweetened flaked
   coconut
Optional: 1 c. chopped walnuts

Combine cracker crumbs, sugar and melted butter in a bowl; mix well. Press crumb mixture into a lightly greased 8"x8" baking pan. Bake at 350 degrees for 20 to 30 minutes, until golden. Let stand until completely cooled. Sprinkle chocolate chips over crust. Evenly drizzle condensed milk over chips. Sprinkle coconut and walnuts, if using, over top. Bake at 350 degrees for 30 minutes longer, or until coconut is golden. Cool completely. Cut into squares. Makes 8 servings.

Whoever wants to know the heart and mind of America had better learn baseball, the rules and realities of the game...and do it by watching first some high school or small-town teams.

—Jacques Barzun

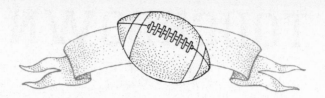

Coconutty Macaroons

Coleen Butts
Amenia, NY

Make these macaroons extra special by placing a spoonful of raspberry jam in the center before baking!

14-oz. pkg. sweetened flaked coconut
14-oz. can sweetened condensed milk

2 t. almond extract
1 egg white
1/8 t. salt

Stir together coconut, condensed milk and extract in a large bowl. In a separate bowl, whisk together egg white and salt until foamy. Stir egg white mixture into coconut mixture. Place mixture by rounded tablespoonfuls onto parchment paper-lined baking sheets. Bake at 325 degrees for 25 to 30 minutes. Makes about 2-1/2 dozen.

Tumbleweeds

Kathy Harris
Valley Center, KS

This sweet and salty concoction has an irresistible taste that we all love. We make them year after year.

12-oz. pkg. white melting chocolate
1 c. butterscotch chips

1 lb. roasted salted peanuts
3 c. shoestring potato sticks, broken into small pieces

Combine melting chocolate and chips in a microwave-safe bowl. Microwave on high setting for 30 seconds; stir. Continue to heat and stir at 30-second intervals until melted. Fold in peanuts and potato sticks. Drop mixture by tablespoonfuls onto sheets of waxed paper; cool completely. Store in airtight containers. Makes about 3 dozen.

TOUCHDOWN
Treats

Brownie-Stuffed Chocolate Chip Cookies

Kristin Turner
Fuquay-Varina, NC

This is a perfect recipe for cookie exchanges. I mean, a chocolate chip cookie that's been stuffed with a brownie? It's two of the best desserts in one!

20-oz. pkg. brownie mix
1/2 c. butter, softened
1/2 c. butter-flavored shortening
1-1/2 c. brown sugar, packed
2 eggs
1 egg yolk

1 T. vanilla extract
2-1/2 c. all-purpose flour
2 t. baking powder
1/2 t. baking soda
1/2 t. salt
3 c. semi-sweet chocolate chips

Prepare brownie mix according to package directions; bake in an 8"x8" baking pan. Cool completely; cut into one-inch squares. In a bowl, beat together butter and shortening with an electric mixer on medium speed until creamy. Add brown sugar to butter mixture; beat until smooth. Add eggs, egg yolk and vanilla; beat until blended. In a separate bowl, sift together flour, baking powder, baking soda and salt. Gradually beat flour mixture into butter mixture until well combined. Fold in chocolate chips. Cover and refrigerate dough for one hour. For each cookie, enclose a brownie square in 1/2 cup cookie dough. Place cookies on parchment paper-lined baking sheets; chill for 15 minutes. Bake at 350 degrees for 18 to 20 minutes, until golden. Cool on pan for 2 minutes; remove to wire racks to cool completely. Makes about 11 large cookies.

Send cookies to college students so they arrive just before final exams...a sure-fire way to make them smile.

Cookie Cupcakes

Lana Rulevish
Ashley, IL

Talk about a match made in heaven! These cookie cupcakes are the best of both worlds...an airy cupcake with a chocolatey cookie center. These are sure to be a favorite addition to your next game-day spread.

1/2 c. butter, softened
6 T. sugar
1/2 c. plus 6 T. brown sugar, packed and divided
2 eggs, divided
1/2 t. vanilla extract

1 c. plus 2 T. all-purpose flour
1/2 t. baking soda
1/2 t. plus 1/8 t. salt, divided
1 c. semi-sweet chocolate chips
1/2 c. chopped walnuts

Combine butter, sugar and 6 tablespoons brown sugar in a large bowl. Beat with an electric mixer on medium speed until light and fluffy. Beat in one egg and vanilla. In a separate bowl, sift together flour, baking soda and 1/2 teaspoon salt. Gradually beat flour mixture into butter mixture until well blended. Fill paper-lined muffin cups 1/2 full. Bake at 350 degrees for 10 minutes, or until cupcake tops are slightly set. Meanwhile, beat together remaining brown sugar, egg and salt until just combined. Fold in chocolate chips and walnuts. Drop chocolate chip mixture by rounded tablespoonfuls into the center of each cupcake. Bake for 10 minutes longer, or until a toothpick inserted near the center tests clean. Cool for 10 minutes in pan; remove to wire racks to cool completely. Makes one dozen.

A heaping plate of cupcakes, cookies or bars makes a delightful (and delicious) centerpiece at a casual gathering with friends... don't forget the napkins!

TOUCHDOWN
Treats

Man-on-the-Moon Cake

Norma Sevigny
Fenton, MO

This recipe with a funny name was given to my mother by a neighbor. I make this yummy cake in the fall after picking apples. It's wonderfully moist, and the black walnuts add a unique taste and crunch.

3 eggs
1/2 c. oil
2 c. all-purpose flour
1/4 t. salt
1 t. baking soda
2 t. cinnamon

2 c. sugar
2 t. vanilla extract
4 c. Jonathan apples, peeled,
   cored and chopped
1 c. black walnuts, chopped

In a bowl, beat together eggs and oil with an electric mixer on medium speed until foamy. In a separate bowl, sift together flour, salt, baking soda and cinnamon. Gradually beat flour mixture into egg mixture. Stir in remaining ingredients; let stand 30 minutes. Pour batter into a greased and floured 13"x9" baking pan. Bake at 350 degrees for 40 minutes, or until a toothpick inserted in the center tests clean. Cool; spread with Lunar Landing Frosting. Serves 12.

Lunar Landing Frosting:

3-oz. pkg. cream cheese,
   softened
1 t. vanilla extract

1-1/2 c. powdered sugar
1/4 c. butter, softened

In a bowl, beat together all ingredients with an electric mixer on medium speed until creamy.

Don't have a cake tester or toothpick on hand? Use a strand of uncooked spaghetti to test cakes!

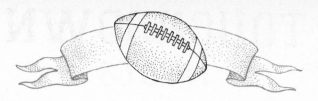

Candy Bar Pie

Stephanie Rhodes
Tishomingo, MS

I found a version of this recipe in a magazine, then I added my own touches. Now I can't go to a family get-together without it!

8-oz. pkg. cream cheese,
　softened
1/2 c. powdered sugar
8-oz. container frozen whipped
　topping, thawed

4 chocolate-covered crispy
　peanut butter candy bars,
　crushed and divided
9-inch graham cracker crust

In a bowl, beat cream cheese with an electric mixer on medium speed until fluffy. Add powdered sugar; beat until well mixed. Fold in whipped topping and half of the crushed candy bar pieces; spoon mixture into crust. Sprinkle remaining crushed candy bar pieces over top; refrigerate for at least 4 hours. Serves 8.

Granny Ruby's Fried Pies

Maranda Croft
Flynn, TX

My granny used to make these wonderful fried pies for us when she had leftover pie crust...so easy to make and sooo delicious.

2 c. all-purpose flour
1/2 t. salt
2/3 c. shortening
1/2 c. buttermilk

1 egg white
21-oz. can favorite-flavor pie
　filling
oil for frying

Sift together flour and salt in a bowl. Cut in shortening until coarse crumbs form. Stir in buttermilk until a dough forms. Refrigerate dough for one hour. Divide dough into 10 balls. Flatten dough into 1/2-inch thick rounds; evenly spoon pie filling onto rounds. Fold rounds in half making a half-moon shape. Seal edges with a fork. Heat 2 inches of oil in a saucepan to 350 degrees. Fry pies, one at a time, until golden, about 3 to 4 minutes on each side. Drain on paper towels. Makes 10.

TOUCHDOWN
Treats

World's Best Cookies

Betty Gretch
Owendale, MN

I took care of an elderly man, and he would make these cookies for me. He was so proud how good they tasted. They were named the World's Best Cookies, and he meant the world to me. I think of that great man every time I make them.

1 c. butter, softened
1 c. oil
1 c. sugar
1 c. brown sugar, packed
1 egg, beaten
3-1/2 c. all-purpose flour
1 t. salt

1 t. baking soda
1 c. quick-cooking oats, uncooked
1 c. crispy rice cereal
1 t. vanilla extract
1 c. sweetened flaked coconut
1/2 c. chopped nuts

In a bowl, beat together butter, oil, sugars and egg with an electric mixer on medium speed until fluffy. Stir in remaining ingredients; mix well. Roll dough into walnut-sized balls. Place cookies on parchment paper-lined baking sheets; flatten balls with a fork. Bake at 350 degrees for 10 to 12 minutes, until golden. Makes about 2 dozen.

Flavoring extracts come in lots of scrumptious flavors besides vanilla like orange, almond, coconut, rum, banana, mango... why not try a different one in your next batch of cookies and bake up a new favorite?

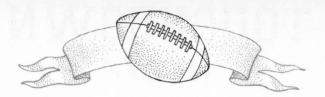

Skillet Cookies

Cheryl Wil
Eglon, WV

These unique cookies aren't baked in the oven, they're prepared in a skillet. Sure, the preparation may be out of the ordinary, but the taste of these little morsels is out of this world!

1/2 c. butter, softened
2 c. sugar
1/2 c. baking cocoa
1/2 c. milk
2 c. corn flake cereal

1/2 c. creamy peanut butter
1 t. vanilla extract
1/2 c. semi-sweet chocolate chips
1/2 c. black walnuts, chopped
1/2 c. sweetened flaked coconut

In a large skillet over medium heat, combine butter, sugar, cocoa and milk. Bring to a boil; cook for 2 minutes. Remove from heat; pour into a heat-proof bowl. Add remaining ingredients; stir to combine. Drop by teaspoonfuls onto wax paper. Let stand for 2 to 3 hours, until set. Makes about 3 dozen.

To clean a cast-iron skillet, simply scrub with coarse salt, wipe with a soft sponge, rinse and pat dry. Salt cleans cast iron thoroughly without damaging the seasoning like dish detergent would.

TOUCHDOWN
Treats

Homemade Vanilla Ice Cream

Jennie Gist
Gooseberry Patch

No one can resist a big bowl of cool, creamy vanilla ice cream on a warm day. No ice cream maker required!

14-oz. can sweetened
  condensed milk

2 T. vanilla extract
2 c. whipping cream

Stir together condensed milk and vanilla in a bowl. In a separate bowl, whip cream with an electric mixer on high speed until stiff peaks form. Fold whipped cream into milk mixture until well combined. Spoon into a 9"x5" loaf pan. Cover and freeze for at least 6 hours, or until firm. Makes about 2 quarts.

Peanutty Ice Cream Roll

Gladys Kielar
Perrysburg, OH

Family & friends are sure to be impressed by this scrumptious dessert. You can use your favorite combinations of ice cream.

1 qt. vanilla ice cream
1 qt. chocolate ice cream
1-1/2 c. peanuts, coarsely
  chopped

Garnish: chocolate syrup

In a chilled bowl, stir vanilla ice cream to soften. Spread on a chilled wax paper-lined 15"x10" jelly-roll pan. Cover and freeze for 2 to 3 hours. Repeat steps with chocolate ice cream, spreading over vanilla ice cream in pan. Cover and freeze for 2 to 3 hours. Starting at a short end, quickly roll up ice cream jelly-roll style, peeling off wax paper as you roll. Roll in peanuts. Wrap with wax paper and freeze until firm. Slice to serve; garnish with chocolate syrup. Serves 10.

For a game-day picnic, fill a
granite-enamel pail with crushed ice
and lots of ice cream treats!

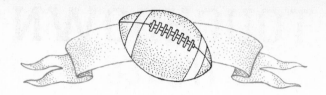

Grandmother's Icebox Cake

Linda Dyczkiewycz
Sagamore Hills, OH

My grandmother hand-wrote a recipe book for me, and this cake was the first entry. Every time I add a little something to it, like sprinkles or peppermints, but I find that the original is still the best.

1/4-oz. env. unflavored gelatin
1/4 c. water
1 c. sugar
1 c. milk
3 pasteurized eggs, separated
1 t. vanilla extract
1/8 t. salt
1 c. whipping cream
1 angel food cake, cubed

Combine gelatin and water in a small bowl; set aside. In a saucepan over medium-low heat, combine sugar, milk and egg yolks. Cook, stirring constantly, until mixture is thickened and coats spoon. Stir in vanilla, salt and gelatin mixture; cool. Meanwhile, beat egg whites with an electric mixer on high speed until soft peaks form. Fold into cooled sugar mixture. Whip cream with an electric mixture on high speed until soft peaks form. Fold half of whipped cream into sugar mixture, reserving half for topping. In a large clear glass bowl or trifle bowl, layer 1/3 of the cake cubes; top with half the sugar mixture. Repeat layers, ending with cake. Spread reserved whipped cream on top; chill before serving. Serves 8 to 10.

Before cubing angel food cake, freeze and then partially thaw it. Fewer crumbs and more to enjoy!

TOUCHDOWN
Treats

Peanut Butter Cheesecake

Monica Reuber
Ludell, KS

To make this extra special, I like to drizzle chocolate across the top and add chopped peanut butter cups.

8-oz. pkg. cream cheese,
  softened
1 c. powdered sugar
1 c. creamy peanut butter
8-oz. container frozen whipped
  topping, thawed

8-inch chocolate cookie crust
Garnish: chocolate syrup,
  chocolate peanut butter cups,
  broken

In a bowl, beat together cream cheese and sugar with an electric mixer on medium speed until fluffy. Beat in peanut butter until smooth. Fold in whipped topping. Spoon mixture into crust. Drizzle with chocolate syrup and sprinkle peanut butter cup pieces over top. Cover and chill until firm. Serves 8.

No-Bake Butterscotch Bars

Janet Wiley
Bonner Springs, KS

These bars are perfect to make on hot days...you don't have to heat up your kitchen by turning the oven on!

2 eggs, beaten
1 c. sugar
2/3 c. margarine
2 c. graham cracker crumbs

2 c. mini marshmallows
1 c. sweetened flaked coconut
1/2 c. creamy peanut butter
11-oz. pkg. butterscotch chips

In a large saucepan over low heat, combine eggs, sugar and margarine. Cook, stirring constantly, for about 5 minutes. Stir in cracker crumbs, marshmallows and coconut; cook until marshmallows are melted. Spread mixture into an ungreased 13"x9" baking pan. Place peanut butter and chips in a microwave-safe bowl. Microwave on high setting for 30 seconds; stir. Repeat until chips are melted and smooth; spread over mixture in pan. Cut into bars while still warm. Makes 14 to 16 bars.

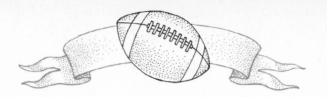

Pumpkin Torte

Linda Meemken
Gilbertville, MA

Mom always made this dessert in the fall, but my family loves it so much I make it year 'round! It takes a little bit of time...but it's worth it!

1-1/2 c. graham cracker crumbs
1/2 c. margarine, melted
2 c. sugar, divided
8-oz. pkg. cream cheese, softened
2 eggs, beaten
3 eggs, separated
15-oz. can pumpkin
1/2 c. milk
1/2 t. salt
1 T. cinnamon
1/4-oz. env. unflavored gelatin
1/4 c. cold water
8-oz. container frozen whipped topping, thawed

Mix together cracker crumbs, margarine and 1/2 cup sugar in a bowl. Press into a lightly greased 13"x9" baking pan; set aside. In a separate bowl, beat together cream cheese, 2 eggs and 3/4 cup sugar with an electric mixer on medium speed until fluffy. Spread cream cheese mixture over crust in pan. Bake at 350 degrees for 20 minutes. Meanwhile, in a saucepan over medium heat, combine 3 egg yolks, pumpkin, milk, salt, cinnamon and 1/2 cup sugar. Cook, stirring constantly, until thickened, about 5 to 10 minutes. Dissolve gelatin in water; add to pumpkin mixture. Remove from heat; cool completely. In a bowl, beat together 3 egg whites and remaining 1/4 cup sugar with an electric mixer on high speed until fluffy. Fold egg white mixture into pumpkin mixture; pour over cream cheese layer. Refrigerate until set. Spread whipped topping over all; refrigerate. Cut into bars to serve. Makes 14 to 16.

Instead of carving your pumpkin this year, why not paint it in your favorite team's colors? You could even paint on their logo or mascot.

STADIUM-SIZED
Recipes for a Crowd

Debbie's Clam Chowder for a Crowd

Debra Jurczyk
Gilbertville, MA

Since we know lots of people who love clam chowder and chowder cook-offs, I decided to come up with my own chowder. This recipe makes a lot, so invite over lots of family & friends!

1-inch cube salt pork, diced
2 c. plus 5 T. butter, divided
5 c. onions, diced
5 c. celery, diced
1 T. dried parsley
1 T. dried marjoram
1 T. dried rosemary
1 t. dried basil
1 t. dried thyme
2-1/2 c. all-purpose flour,
    divided

48-oz. can clam broth
4 lbs. fresh or frozen clams,
    chopped and juice reserved
2 45-oz. cans chopped clams,
    drained and juice reserved
12 lbs. red potatoes, peeled and
    cut into bite-size pieces
1 T. white pepper
1 qt. half-and-half
1 T. sea salt

Cook salt pork until crisp in a very large stockpot over medium heat; drain. Melt 5 tablespoons butter in the same stockpot. Sauté onions and celery until translucent. Add herbs and 1/2 cup flour; stir to combine. In a saucepan over medium-high heat, combine clam broth and reserved clam juice; heat to boiling. Pour clam broth mixture into onion mixture; stir. Place potatoes into stockpot; add pepper. Cover and cook over high heat for 20 minutes, or until potatoes are fork-tender. Meanwhile, in a separate saucepan over medium heat, combine remaining butter and flour. Cook, whisking constantly, until mixture thickens and starts to turn golden. Add butter mixture and clams to stockpot. Reduce heat to medium; cook for 15 minutes. Add half-and-half and salt; cook for 10 minutes more without boiling. Makes about 6 gallons.

Spoon chowder into a thermos and bring it along to the high school football games...a scrumptious way to warm up at half-time!

STADIUM-SIZED
Recipes for a Crowd

Michelle's Chicken Strata

Michelle Fredrick
Brookville, OH

This recipe has been in my family for generations. It is a wonderful, tummy-warming dish for brunch or supper...so filling and satisfying.

10 c. bread, cut into
    1/2-inch cubes
2 c. cooked chicken, diced
1 c. potato, peeled and diced
1 c. carrots, peeled and diced
1 c. celery, diced
1/4 c. fresh parsley, minced
4 c. milk

2-1/2 c. chicken broth
5 eggs, beaten
1/4 c. butter, melted and cooled
1 t. salt
1/2 t. pepper
2 12-oz. jars chicken gravy,
    warmed

Arrange bread cubes in a single layer on several ungreased large baking sheets. Bake at 350 degrees for 20 to 30 minutes, until crisp and golden. Transfer bread cubes to a large bowl. Add chicken, potato, carrots, celery and parsley; set aside. In a separate large bowl, combine milk, broth, eggs, butter, salt and pepper. Pour milk mixture over bread mixture and toss to coat. Transfer to 2 greased 13"x9" baking pans. Bake, uncovered, at 350 degrees for 45 minutes; stir. Bake an additional 45 minutes, or until a knife inserted in the center comes out clean. Serve with warmed chicken gravy. Serves 12 to 14.

Liven up plain orange juice with a splash of sparkling white grape juice and serve in decorative glasses with curly ribbons in team colors!

Jalapeño Pepper Poppers

Gwen Schroeder
LeClaire, IA

*This is one of the best popper recipes around! They are always
gone in no time...scrumptious at any gathering.*

8-oz. pkg. cream cheese,
   softened
1 c. shredded sharp Cheddar
   cheese
1 c. shredded Monterey Jack
   cheese
6 slices bacon, crisply cooked
   and crumbled

1/2 t. chili powder
1/4 t. garlic powder
1 lb. jalapeño peppers, halved
   lengthwise and seeded
1/2 c. dry bread crumbs

Combine cheeses, bacon and seasonings in a bowl; mix well. Spoon
one to 2 tablespoons cheese mixture into each pepper half. Roll cheese-
filled peppers in bread crumbs. Place peppers, filled-side up, in a greased
15"x10" jelly-roll pan. Bake, uncovered, at 300 degrees for 20 minutes.
Makes about 2 dozen.

Seed jalapeño peppers in a snap with a vegetable peeler.
Just cut the top off the pepper, insert the peeler and use a
circular motion to remove the seeds and ribs...so easy!

STADIUM-SIZED
Recipes for a Crowd

Mexican Pizza Dip

Nadeen Lough
New Ulm, MN

Everyone who's ever tried this dip loves it! I always get asked for the recipe or have to bring it to the next get-together.

1-1/2 lbs. ground beef
1-1/4 oz. pkg. taco seasoning
   mix
2 16-oz. cans refried beans
12-oz. container guacamole
16-oz. container sour cream

4 c. shredded Cheddar cheese
Garnish: chopped tomato,
   shredded lettuce, sliced black
   olives, chopped green onions
scoop-style corn chips or tortilla
   chips

Brown beef in a skillet over medium heat; drain. Add taco seasoning to beef and cook according to package directions. Spread beans in a lightly greased 12" deep-dish pizza pan. Top beans with beef mixture. In a bowl, mix together guacamole and sour cream. Spoon guacamole mixture over beef mixture. Sprinkle with cheese. Garnish with desired veggies. Serve with chips. Serves 12 to 15.

Make your game-day celebration easier by making your dips and spreads in advance...they're usually fine in the fridge for up to three days, and the flavor may be even better!

Grammy's Trio Pasta

Maria Maxey
Davenport, FL

This quick & delicious pasta salad is a must at cookouts and picnics.
The dressing tastes wonderful on salads and Italian sandwiches too!

12-oz. box tri-color rotini pasta,
    uncooked
1 red pepper, chopped
1 green pepper, chopped
1 zucchini, chopped
8-oz. can sliced black olives,
    drained

1 red onion, chopped
1 c. cherry tomatoes, halved
8-oz. pkg. crumbled fat-free
    feta cheese
Garnish: fresh basil leaves

Cook pasta according to package directions; drain and rinse with cold water. Combine all ingredients except feta cheese and garnish in a large bowl; toss to mix well. Pour Pasta Salad Dressing over mixture; stir to coat well. Fold in feta cheese; garnish with basil. Makes 10 to 12 servings.

Pasta Salad Dressing:

1/2 c. extra-virgin olive oil
1/3 c. cider vinegar
2 T. balsamic vinegar
2 T. honey

2 T. Italian seasoning
1 t. red pepper flakes
1/4 t. cayenne pepper
1/2 t. sea salt

Whisk together all ingredients in a bowl.

Combine ingredients for homemade salad dressing in a squeeze bottle instead of a bowl. Shake bottle to incorporate flavors and squeeze onto salad...what could be easier?

Buetow's Mini Cheese Balls

Susan Buetow
Du Quoin, IL

These are my hubby's favorite appetizer. The recipe was shared by a friend in our congregation.

8-oz. pkg. cream cheese,
  softened
1 green onion, chopped
1/2 t. seasoned salt

1/4 t. Worcestershire sauce
Optional: 1/4 t. dry mustard
1/4 c. chopped pecans
2-1/4 oz. jar dried, chipped beef

Mix together all the ingredients except beef. Roll cream cheese mixture into nickel-size balls. Finely chop beef. Roll balls in beef to coat. Refrigerate until ready to serve. Makes about 20 balls.

Traci's Easy Hashbrown Casserole

Melissa Knight
Athens, AL

My dear friend Traci gave me this recipe after she brought these yummy potatoes to work. The casserole is so delicious we made at least 20 copies of the recipe to share!

1 c. onion, finely diced
1 t. seasoned salt
salt and pepper to taste
26-oz. can cream of chicken soup

1 c. butter, melted
4 c. shredded Cheddar cheese
30-oz. pkg. frozen shredded
  hashbrowns, partially thawed

In a bowl, mix together onion and seasonings. Stir in soup, butter and cheese; fold in hashbrowns. Transfer mixture to a greased 13"x9" baking pan. Bake, uncovered, at 350 degrees for 45 minutes, or until golden and bubbly. Makes 8 to 10 servings.

Mini Cheesecakes

Michele Elli
Palm Harbor, Fl

Here is one of my favorite cheesecake recipes, given to me by one of my sisters. I like it because it is so fast, so easy and so good. Top with fresh fruit, canned pie filling, chocolate sauce or preserves... be creative!

12 vanilla wafers	1/2 c. sugar
2 8-oz. pkgs. cream cheese, softened	1 t. vanilla extract
	2 eggs

Line a muffin tin with aluminum foil muffin cups. Place a vanilla wafer in each cup. In a bowl, beat together cream cheese, sugar and vanilla with an electric mixer on medium speed until fluffy. Add eggs, one at a time, beating after each addition, until well blended. Spoon cream cheese mixture over wafers, filling cups 3/4 full. Bake at 325 degrees for 25 minutes; let cool. Makes 12 mini cheesecakes.

Delectable fruit like peaches needn't go to waste if it ripens quicker than you can eat it. Purée it, freeze and use later for topping cheesecake or waffles.

STADIUM-SIZED
Recipes for a Crowd

Mini Pie Bites

Krissy Mosqueda
Houston, TX

This is one of my favorite desserts! I love that you can customize it and make a dozen different flavors if you want to. It's quick, easy, delicious and most of all, FUN!

15-oz. pkg. frozen pie crusts, thawed
1 c. favorite-flavor pie filling

1 T. milk
1/2 c. powdered sugar

Unroll pie crusts. Cut each crust into 12 equal squares. Place one to 2 teaspoons of pie filling into the center of each crust square. Bring 4 corners of crust together above filling; pinch together corners and seams to seal. Place mini pies into ungreased muffin cups, one pie per cup. Bake at 450 degrees for 11 to 14 minutes, until golden; cool. Meanwhile, in a bowl, slowly whisk milk into powdered sugar until a glaze consistency is reached. Using a fork, drizzle glaze over bites. Let stand for about 20 minutes. Makes 2 dozen.

Whip up some homemade cherry pie filling in no time. Just combine one pound pitted tart cherries, 3/4 cup sugar, 1/3 cup cornstarch and 2 tablespoons lemon juice in a saucepan over medium heat. Bring to a boil, then simmer until thickened...so simple!

Iced Coffee Punch

Peggy Giese
Barrigada, Guam

*We've made this for so many years, long before frappuccinos and
iced coffee were fashionable. It's always been a favorite.*

1 c. instant coffee granules
2-1/2 c. sugar
4 c. boiling water
1/2 gal. vanilla ice cream
1/2 gal. chocolate ice cream

1/2 gal. coffee ice cream
3 gals. milk
16-oz. container frozen whipped
   topping, thawed
Garnish: chocolate sprinkles

Dissolve coffee granules and sugar in boiling water; chill. Divide cooled
coffee mixture, ice creams and milk between two 3-gallon punch bowls.
Top punch with whipped topping, spreading with a spatula. Garnish
with sprinkles. Serve immediately. Makes 50 servings.

A punch bowl is a festive touch that makes even the simplest
beverage special! Surround it with baseballs and baseball cards
or mini footballs and helmets for some game-day cheer.

STADIUM-SIZED
Recipes for a Crowd

Game-Time TV Mix

Sara Klauer
Coal Valley, IL

My grandmother used to make this mix for big game-day gatherings. We would always sit in front of the television, watching the game, chatting and munching on this mix. Now that she has passed, my brother and I take turns making it.

6 c. bite-size crispy rice cereal squares
6 c. regular or honey-nut doughnut-shaped oat cereal
5 c. pretzel sticks
1 to 2 lbs. cashews
3/4 c. butter, melted
1 T. garlic salt
2 to 3 T. Worcestershire sauce

Combine cereals, pretzels and cashews in a deep 13"x9" aluminum foil baking pan. Drizzle melted butter over cereal mixture; toss to coat. Sprinkle with garlic salt and Worcestershire sauce; mix well. Bake, uncovered, at 325 degrees for 45 minutes to one hour, stirring every 15 minutes, until golden. Cool completely; store in an airtight container. Makes 20 to 25 servings.

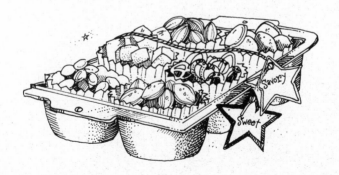

Paper baking cups are perfect for serving up party-size scoops of nuts or snack mix. They come in lots of colors and patterns too...you're sure to find one to suit your occasion.

10-Layer Taco Dip

Amanda Bowden
Bangor, ME

My whole family loves this yummy dip. Serve with bowls of your favorite chips and veggies. Try some colorful tortilla chips made from blue or red corn...deliciously different!

31-oz. can refried beans
2 lbs. ground beef
1-1/4 oz. pkg. taco seasoning
  mix
8-oz. pkg. cream cheese,
  softened
16-oz. container sour cream
24-oz. jar salsa
2 to 3 tomatoes, chopped

1 onion, chopped
2 green peppers, chopped
8-oz. pkg. shredded lettuce
8-oz. pkg. shredded Mexican-
  blend cheese
2 2-1/4 oz. cans sliced black
  olives
Optional: sliced jalapeño peppers,
  corn, black beans

Spread beans in a lightly greased 13"x11" aluminum foil baking pan; set aside. Brown beef in a skillet over medium heat; drain. Add taco seasoning to beef and cook according to package directions. Let cool; spread over bean layer. In a bowl, mix together cream cheese and sour cream; spoon over beef. Top with remaining ingredients in order given. Arrange jalapeños, corn and black beans over top, if desired. Cover with aluminum foil and refrigerate for at least one hour to overnight. Serves 25.

A dip buffet will be fun at your next get-together! Have plenty of chips, crackers, sliced veggies, bread rounds and pita triangles on hand. Get creative and serve your dips in unexpected serving "dishes" such as hollowed-out vegetables and breads.

STADIUM-SIZED
Recipes for a Crowd

Bacon-Potato Chowder

Diana Leischner
Monticello, IL

This is an easy recipe to feed a crowd. Everyone always loves it.

12 slices bacon, diced
2 onions, chopped
6 stalks celery, sliced
12 potatoes, peeled and diced
2/3 c. butter
1 c. all-purpose flour
1/2 gal. milk

2 carrots, peeled and shredded
1 T. salt
1 t. pepper
Garnish: shredded Cheddar
    cheese, chopped green
    onions, sour cream

Cook bacon until crisp in a skillet over medium heat; drain, reserving drippings in skillet. Sauté onion and celery in drippings until crisp-tender; drain. Place potatoes in a Dutch oven and cover with water. Bring to a boil and cook 20 minutes, or until tender. Drain and set aside. Melt butter in the same Dutch oven. Stir in flour until smooth. Gradually add milk. Bring to a boil; cook and stir for 2 minutes, or until thickened. Reduce heat; add onion mixture, potatoes, carrots, salt and pepper. Cook 10 minutes or until heated through. Sprinkle with bacon. Garnish as desired. Serves 12 to 14.

Spice up Bacon-Potato Soup with crushed tortilla chips, shredded Pepper Jack cheese and chopped jalapeño peppers.

Vegetable Beef Soup for 50

Shirl Parsons
Cape Carteret, NC

This is a great soup to bring to a tailgating party. Bowls of this hearty soup, paired with slices of crusty bread, will keep all the fans cheering.

8 lbs. boneless beef chuck roast, cut into 1/2-inch cubes
1 c. all-purpose flour
1 T. salt
2 t. pepper
1/2 c. oil
4 cloves garlic, minced
2 bay leaves
2 t. dried thyme
6 qts. water
4 15-oz. cans tomato sauce

46-oz. can tomato juice
12 cubes beef bouillon
2 c. pearled barley, uncooked
2 lbs. potatoes, peeled and cubed
1-1/2 lbs. carrots, peeled and sliced
1 lb. cabbage, chopped
1 lb. onion, chopped
2 c. fresh or frozen green beans
2 c. fresh or frozen peas

In a very large bowl, toss beef with flour, salt and pepper. Heat oil in a large Dutch oven. Working in batches, brown beef in oil; transfer beef to a large stockpot. Add remaining ingredients except vegetables to beef; bring to a boil. Reduce heat to low; cover and simmer for one hour. Add vegetables to soup; return to a boil. Return heat to low; cover and simmer for an additional 1-1/2 to 2 hours, until vegetables are cooked and beef is tender. Remove bay leaves before serving. Serves 50.

Add zest to a favorite chili or vegetable soup recipe in a jiffy!
Just stir in a generous amount of spicy salsa.

STADIUM-SIZED
Recipes for a Crowd

Slow-Cooker Beef & Bean Burritos

Lynda McCormick
Burkburnett, TX

It's heavenly to come home to the smell of these burritos cooking away in the slow cooker. These are perfect for parties and get-togethers...easy to make for a crowd!

2-lb. beef flank steak
1-1/4 oz. pkg. taco seasoning
   mix
1 c. sweet onion, chopped
1 T. cider vinegar
4-1/2 oz. can chopped green
   chiles

16-oz. can fat-free refried beans
12 8-inch flour tortillas
1-1/2 c. shredded Monterey Jack
   cheese
1-1/2 c. roma tomatoes, chopped
3/4 c. fat-free sour cream

Trim any fat from beef; rub all sides with taco seasoning. Place beef in a large slow cooker that has been sprayed with non-stick vegetable spray. Add onion, vinegar and chiles to slow cooker. Cover and cook on low setting for 9 hours. Remove beef from slow cooker; shred with 2 forks. Return shredded beef to slow cooker. Warm beans according to package directions. Spread 2 tablespoons of beans in the center of each tortilla. Top beans with 1/3 cup of beef mixture from slow cooker. Sprinkle with cheese and tomatoes; dollop with a tablespoon of sour cream. Roll up tightly. Makes one dozen servings.

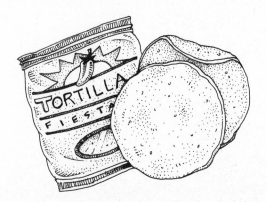

A basket of warmed flour tortillas is a must-have with burritos and fajitas. Simply wrap tortillas in aluminum foil and pop into a 250-degree oven for about 15 minutes...easy!

Norma's Fumi Salad

Norma Chavira
West Covina, CA

This Oriental twist on coleslaw is a welcome change from the ordinary. The ramen noodles and almonds add a yummy crunch, while the seasoned rice vinegar provides a flavorful bite.

2 16-oz. pkgs. coleslaw mix	3-oz. pkg. ramen noodles
4 green onions, chopped	1/4 c. sliced almonds, toasted
1 bunch cilantro, finely chopped	1 T. toasted sesame seeds

In a bowl, combine coleslaw mix, green onions and cilantro; toss well. Crush ramen noodles; discard seasoning packet. Just before serving, toss crushed noodles, almonds and sesame seed into coleslaw. Drizzle with Dressing; mix well until evenly coated. Makes 18 to 20 servings.

Dressing:

1/2 c. oil	1 t. salt
3 T. seasoned rice vinegar	1/2 t. pepper
2 T. sugar	Optional: 1 t. flavor enhancer

Whisk together all ingredients in a bowl.

Bags of salad mix and coleslaw mix are real time-savers. Keep opened bags crispy by storing in airtight containers or plastic zipping bags...just be sure to press out all the air before refrigerating.

STADIUM-SIZED
Recipes for a Crowd

Game-Day Dim Sum

Carly St. Clair
Lynnwood, WA

My husband John and son Greg are learning Chinese together. Adding some Chinese home cooking to your game-day feast will be good eats and good memories! If you don't have any chili oil, you can substitute red pepper flakes.

2 lbs. ground beef
1 T. fresh ginger, peeled and
    grated
1 T. garlic, minced
1 T. soy sauce
1 T. white wine or chicken broth
1 t. chili oil

3 green onions, chopped
1/2 red onion, diced
1 T. cornstarch
salt and pepper to taste
48 wonton wrappers
Garnish: additional soy sauce
    for dipping

In a bowl, combine all ingredients except wonton wrappers and garnish; mix well. Place one tablespoon beef mixture into the center of each wrapper. Bring corners of wrapper together above beef mixture and twist, sealing edges. Place wontons in a steamer that has been sprayed with non-stick vegetable spray. Steam on high setting for 20 to 30 minutes, until beef mixture is cooked through. Serve with soy sauce for dipping. Makes 16 servings.

Make your own chili oil in no time. Just combine 1/4 cup olive oil and one teaspoon red pepper flakes in a saucepan over low heat. Cook for about 5 minutes, then cool. Store, refrigerated, in an airtight container for up to ten days.

Little Sugar Piggies

Candace Head
Haleyville, AL

*Warning! You can't eat just one of these scrumptious
little treats...plus, it's such an easy slow-cooker recipe.*

30 hot dogs
2 lbs. bacon
wooden toothpicks

16-oz. pkg. light brown sugar
Optional: 3 to 4 shakes hot
    pepper sauce

Cut hot dogs and bacon slices into 3 to 4 equal pieces each. Wrap each
hot dog piece with a piece of bacon; secure with a toothpick. Transfer
wrapped hot dogs to a slow cooker. Add brown sugar and hot sauce,
if using, to slow cooker. Cover and cook on low setting, stirring
occasionally, for 5 to 6 hours, until bacon is cooked. Serves 25 to 30.

Bacon-Wrapped Water Chestnuts

Deborah Desrocher
Methuen, MA

To put it bluntly...these are just plain good!

1 lb. bacon
2 8-oz. cans whole water
    chestnuts, drained

wooden toothpicks
Garnish: catsup

Cut bacon slices in half. Wrap each water chestnut with a piece of
bacon; secure with a toothpick. Place water chestnuts on a baking
sheet. Bake at 350 degrees for one hour, or until bacon is crisp. Top
each wrapped chestnut with a dollop of catsup. Serves 20 to 25.

Put new, large terra cotta
saucers to use as picnic
serving bowls...just line
with wax paper.

STADIUM-SIZED
Recipes for a Crowd

Mom's Wacky Cake

Sandy Unrein
Littleton, CO

My mom always made this cake...it's so simple. The texture is between a cake and a brownie, and it needs absolutely no frosting. The flavor improves as the days go by, plus, it's fun to make with the kids!

3 c. cake flour
2 c. sugar
6 T. baking cocoa
2 t. baking soda
1 t. salt

3/4 c. oil
2 T. white vinegar
2 t. vanilla extract
2 c. water

Sift together flour, sugar, cocoa, baking soda and salt in an ungreased 13"x9" baking pan. Make 3 wells in flour mixture. Add oil to one well, vinegar to another well and vanilla to the remaining well. Drizzle water over all; mix well. Bake at 350 degrees for 35 minutes, or until a toothpick inserted in the center tests clean. Makes 16 servings.

Vintage tin cake carriers are so pretty...their colors and patterns add a spot of cheer to kitchens and get-togethers! Keep an eye out for them at flea markets, tag sales and rummage sales.

Ice Cream Sandwich Dessert

Ann Crane
Pleasant Garden, NC

This yummy recipe was given to me by my friend Doris.
She's one of the best cooks I know. It's like an ice cream
sundae...only sliced and eaten like a cake.

24 ice cream sandwiches,
   unwrapped
16-oz. container frozen whipped
   topping, thawed
1/3 to 1/2 c. pineapple or
   strawberry ice cream topping

Garnish: caramel topping,
   chocolate syrup, chopped
   nuts, maraschino cherries

Place 12 ice cream sandwiches in a single layer in a 13"x11" aluminum foil baking pan. Spread half of whipped topping over sandwiches. Drizzle pineapple or strawberry topping over whipped topping. Place remaining sandwiches on top; spread with remaining whipped topping. Garnish with caramel topping, chocolate syrup, nuts and cherries. Freeze until serving. Cut into squares. Serves 24 to 28.

Cake doughnuts make a yummy ice cream sandwich.
Cut a doughnut in half and add a scoop of softened ice cream
between the two halves. Place on a baking sheet and
freeze for one hour...tasty!

STADIUM-SIZED
Recipes for a Crowd

Nan's Chipped Beef & Pimento Cheese Ball

Nancy Rossman
Port Richey, FL

I bring this savory appetizer to every get-together. Sometimes just for some variety, I'll roll one ball in chipped beef and the other ball in some chopped walnuts...it's delicious either way!

2 8-oz. pkgs. cream cheese, softened
4-oz. jar diced pimentos, drained
1/2 lb. dried, chipped beef, chopped and divided
1 bunch green onions, chopped

8-oz. pkg. finely shredded Cheddar cheese
Worcestershire sauce to taste
crackers and sliced veggies for dipping

In a bowl, mix together all ingredients except crackers and veggies, reserving 1/2 cup beef. Blend well. Form mixture into 2 equal balls. Wrap balls in plastic wrap and refrigerate for at least one hour to overnight. Before serving, roll balls in reserved beef to coat. Serve with crackers and vegetables. Serves 16 to 20.

For tasty fun at your next game-day party, turn any favorite cheese ball recipe into a football. Just shape, sprinkle with paprika and pipe on sour cream or cream cheese "laces."

Floorboard Bean Dip

Mindy Munchel
Greensburg, IN

On the way to a family gathering, a big dish of this dip got knocked off the seat and spilled all over the floorboard. Now when we go anywhere, I'm asked to bring the famous Floorboard Bean Dip!

1 lb. ground beef
1 c. catsup
3/4 c. brown sugar, packed
1 green pepper, chopped
1 onion, chopped
salt and pepper to taste

28-oz. can baked beans
2 15-1/2 oz. cans mild chili
    beans, drained and rinsed
Worcestershire sauce to taste
3 to 4 slices bacon
tortilla chips

Brown beef in a skillet over medium heat. Drain and add beef to a slow cooker. Stir catsup, brown sugar, green pepper, onion, salt and pepper into beef. Mix in baked beans and chili beans. Season with Worcestershire sauce; stir in bacon slices. Cover and cook on high setting for 30 minutes to one hour, until heated through and bubbly. Remove bacon before serving. Serve with tortilla chips for dipping. Serves 25 to 30.

Keep an eye out at flea markets for woolly blankets.
They make perfect tailgating tablecloths, and will keep you
toasty warm during a chilly Friday night game!

STADIUM-SIZED
Recipes for a Crowd

Easy French Dip Sandwiches

Kathleen White
Bedford, VA

My husband is the pastor of our church, and we regularly host big meals for our congregation and friends. These slow-cooker sandwiches are one of our newest favorites.

4 lbs. stew beef cubes
2 onions
4 cloves garlic, peeled
2 10-1/2 oz. cans beef
   consommé

4 c. water
4 t. beef bouillon granules
18 to 20 crusty rolls or sandwich
   buns, split

Combine all ingredients except rolls or buns in a large slow cooker. Cover and cook on low setting for 8 to 10 hours, until beef is very tender. Remove onions and garlic; discard. Shred beef with 2 forks. Place servings of beef on rolls or buns; serve with cups of juice from the slow cooker for dipping. Serves 18 to 20.

Game-Day Meatballs

Missy Abbott
Hickory, PA

I have been making this tasty game-day recipe for many years. So quick & easy, my family asks for it during the entire football and hockey season!

3 lbs. frozen meatballs
16-oz. jar chili sauce
16-oz. can jellied cranberry sauce

1/4 c. brown sugar, packed
1/4 c. white vinegar

Arrange meatballs on lightly greased rimmed baking sheets; bake at 350 degrees for 20 to 25 minutes, until browned. Transfer meatballs to a slow cooker; stir in remaining ingredients. Cover and cook on high setting, stirring occasionally, for one to 2 hours. Makes 15 to 20 servings.

Easy Huevos Rancheros Casserole
Jen Licon-Conner
Gooseberry Patch

This convenient one-dish casserole is perfect for breakfast, brunch or dinner. If you're a little more daring, add a spicy kick by chopping up a jalapeño pepper and adding it to the eggs.

32-oz. pkg. frozen diced
  potatoes, thawed
1 doz. eggs
1 c. milk
1-1/2 t. dried oregano
1-1/2 t. ground cumin
1/2 t. chili powder

1/4 t. garlic powder
8-oz. pkg. shredded Mexican-
  blend cheese
16-oz. jar thick and chunky salsa
8-oz. container sour cream
Garnish: chopped fresh cilantro

Place potatoes in a lightly greased 3-quart casserole dish; set aside. In a bowl, whisk together eggs, milk and seasonings. Pour egg mixture over potatoes. Bake, uncovered, at 375 degrees for 35 to 40 minutes, until a knife inserted in the center tests clean. Sprinkle cheese over egg mixture; bake for an additional 3 minutes, or until cheese is melted. Let stand 10 minutes before serving. Top with salsa, sour cream and cilantro; cut into squares to serve. Serves 12.

Pop bottles from your Mexican grocer make perfect
vases for colorful flowers.

Bunch for Brunch Eggs

Sharon Tillman
Hampton, VA

This delicious breakfast bake can be prepared the night before and refrigerated until ready to cook. All you'll have to do is lengthen the cooking time by about 15 minutes...so easy!

3 doz. eggs
1/4 c. milk
1/2 c. butter
1/2 c. cooking sherry or water
2-oz. jar diced pimentos, drained
8-oz. pkg. sliced mushrooms

2 T. green pepper, chopped
2 10-3/4 oz. cans cream of
  mushroom soup
8-oz. pkg. shredded sharp
  Cheddar cheese
paprika to taste

In a very large bowl, whisk together eggs and milk. Melt butter in a very large skillet. Scramble eggs in butter until almost set. Stir sherry or water and vegetables into eggs. Transfer half of egg mixture to a greased 3-quart casserole dish. Top eggs in dish with half each of soup and cheese; repeat layers. Sprinkle with paprika. Bake, uncovered, at 250 degrees for one hour, or until heated through and eggs are fully set. Serves 15 to 20.

Not sure if you have a bad egg? A good test is to hold it close to your ear and give it a light shake. If you hear any sloshing sounds, it's probably best to throw that egg out.

Baked Cheesy Chicken Penne

Kelsey Majors
Norman, OK

*This is an ideal recipe to use up leftover grilled chicken or ham.
It's a perfect dish to take to a potluck or get-together, because
who doesn't love a dressed-up mac & cheese?*

16-oz. pkg. penne pasta,
  uncooked
2 c. milk
2 c. half-and-half
1 lb. American cheese, shredded
1/2 c. green onions, chopped

2 c. grilled chicken, chopped
1 t. salt
1 t. pepper
1/2 c. shredded Cheddar cheese
1/2 c. dry bread crumbs

Cook pasta according to package directions; drain and set aside. In a
saucepan over medium heat, bring milk and half-and-half to a boil.
Remove from heat and slowly whisk in American cheese until melted
and smooth. In a large bowl, stir together cooked pasta, cheese mixture,
green onions, chicken, salt and pepper. Spoon mixture into a lightly
greased 13"x9" baking pan; sprinkle Cheddar cheese and bread crumbs
over top. Bake, covered with aluminum foil, at 350 degrees for
30 minutes. Uncover and bake an additional 15 minutes, or until
cheese is melted and bubbly. Serves 10 to 12.

Whenever you're grilling chicken
for dinner, toss a few extra boneless,
skinless chicken breasts on the grill.
Sliced and refrigerated, they can
be served another day in sandwich
wraps, over pasta or topping a
hearty salad for an easy meal
with fresh-grilled flavor.

STADIUM-SIZED
Recipes for a Crowd

Jalapeño Popper Dip

Marceen Hernandez
Worland, WY

This spicy dip tastes just like a jalapeño popper!

2 8-oz. pkgs. cream cheese,
  softened
1 c. mayonnaise
4-oz. can sliced jalapeño peppers,
  drained and diced

4-oz. can diced green chiles
1/4 c. shredded Cheddar cheese
1/2 c. shredded Parmesan cheese
1/4 c. dry bread crumbs
assorted crackers and chips

In a bowl, mix together all ingredients except Parmesan cheese, bread crumbs and crackers or chips. Spoon mixture into an ungreased 13"x9" baking pan. Sprinkle Parmesan cheese and bread crumbs over top. Bake, uncovered, at 350 degrees for 25 to 30 minutes, until bubbly and golden. Serve warm with crackers and chips for dipping. Serves 20 to 25.

Chili con Queso

Carole Rhoades
Galena, OH

When I was a kid, my mom used to make this slow-cooker recipe for special occasions. It makes a lot and is always a crowd-pleaser.

1 lb. ground pork sausage
1 lb. ground beef
32-oz. pkg. pasteurized process
  cheese spread, cubed

10-oz. can diced tomatoes with
  green chiles
tortilla chips

Brown sausage and beef in a large skillet over medium heat; drain. Combine meat and remaining ingredients in a slow cooker. Cover and cook on high setting, stirring occasionally, for 1-1/2 to 2 hours, until cheese is melted and dip is smooth. Serve with chips. Serves 20 to 25.

Sausage Pizza-Stuffed Mushrooms

Linda Robson
Boston, MA

I was trying to think of something new and fun to bring to a potluck, and then it hit me! I love stuffed mushrooms and pizza, so why not combine the two? The result was a huge hit...everyone wanted my recipe!

1/2 lb. ground Italian pork
    sausage
16-oz. pkg. whole mushrooms
1/2 c. onion, chopped
2 cloves garlic, crushed
1/4 c. dry bread crumbs

2 T. fresh parsley, chopped
1/4 c. grated Parmesan cheese
1/4 c. shredded mozzarella
    cheese
1/4 c. pizza or spaghetti sauce

Cook sausage in a skillet over medium heat until browned; drain, reserving one teaspoon drippings in pan. Remove stems from mushroom caps. Chop stems. Place caps on a lightly greased baking sheet; set aside. Sauté onion, garlic and chopped stems in drippings until tender. Combine sausage and onion mixture in a bowl; stir in remaining ingredients except mushroom caps. Evenly divide sausage mixture between mushroom caps. Bake at 400 degrees for 20 minutes, or until heated through and tender. Makes 20 servings.

Store unwashed, dry mushrooms in the refrigerator. The mushrooms will stay fresher longer if they're placed in a paper bag rather than a plastic bag.

STADIUM-SIZED
Recipes for a Crowd

Five Pounds of Fudge

Heather Roberts
Quebec, Canada

I was lucky to obtain one of my grandmother's most treasured cookbooks when she passed on. It's a treat exploring the old-fashioned recipes, and this fudge recipe has since become everyone's most-wanted sweet treat!

2 12-oz. pkgs. semi-sweet
   chocolate chips
1 c. butter, softened
7-oz. jar marshmallow creme

12-oz. can evaporated milk
4-1/2 c. brown sugar, packed
2 T. vanilla extract
Optional: 1 to 2 c. chopped nuts

In a bowl, combine chocolate chips, butter and marshmallow creme; set aside. Combine milk and sugar in a heavy saucepan over medium-high heat. Cook until mixture comes to a rolling boil. Boil, stirring constantly, for 8 minutes. Pour milk mixture into chocolate mixture; stir until well mixed and chips are melted. Beat with an electric mixer on medium speed until fudge is thickened and no longer shiny. Beat in vanilla and nuts, if using. Spoon fudge evenly into a greased 15"x10" jelly-roll pan; refrigerate until chilled. Cut into small squares before serving. Store in an airtight container. Makes 5 dozen.

Pile squares of scrumptious fudge under a clear glass dome...oh-so inviting for guests to sample!

Coconut Crunch Pretzel Bars

Gloria Suciu
Pensacola, FL

I make these scrumptious salty-sweet bars every year for special occasions. They're my daughter's favorite dessert! You won't be able to eat just one.

15-1/4 oz. pkg. German
   chocolate cake mix
1/2 c. pretzels, crushed
1/2 c. butter, melted
3 eggs, divided
1/4 c. sugar

1 c. dark corn syrup
1 c. pecans, chopped
1 c. butterscotch chips
2-1/4 c. sweetened flaked
   coconut
1 c. semi-sweet chocolate chips

In a large bowl, combine dry cake mix, pretzels, butter and one egg. Beat with an electric mixer on low speed until well blended. Press mixture into a 13"x9" baking pan that has been lined with aluminum foil and sprayed with non-stick vegetable spray. Bake at 350 degrees for 15 minutes, or until crust puffs up and is dry. Cool 5 minutes. Meanwhile, combine sugar, corn syrup and remaining 2 eggs in a bowl. Beat with an electric mixer on low speed until well blended; fold in remaining ingredients. Spoon filling evenly over partially baked crust. Bake for 30 to 40 minutes longer, until edges are golden and center is almost set. Let cool one hour before slicing into bars. Makes 3 dozen.

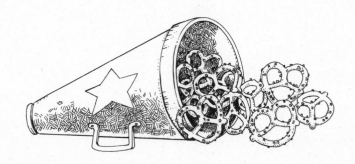

Giant megaphones are great for serving grab & go snacks like popcorn, pretzels or chips. Just lay them on the party table and fill...a snap!

STADIUM-SIZED
Recipes for a Crowd

Frosty Banana Punch

Patti Wafford
Mount Vernon, TX

This is my favorite punch recipe! A friend of mine makes this for lots of get-togethers because everyone loves it.

4 c. sugar
6 c. water
46-oz. can pineapple juice

6 bananas, mashed
2 qts. ginger ale, chilled

Bring sugar and water to a boil in a saucepan over medium heat. Boil for 5 minutes; remove from heat and cool. Stir in juice and bananas. Pour into a large freezer-safe bowl. Freeze for 2 to 3 hours before serving. To serve, combine banana mixture and ginger ale in a large punchbowl. Serves 18 to 24.

Margarita Punch

Janis Greene
Brandon, FL

If you prefer, you can omit the alcohol and have your guests serve themselves. Set the tequila bottle next to the punch bowl with a shot glass and let them decide.

2 12-oz. cans frozen limeade
    concentrate, thawed
12-oz. can frozen lemonade
    concentrate, thawed

1-oz. bottle orange extract
4 c. water
3 ltrs. lemon-lime soda, chilled
1-1/2 c. tequila

Combine all ingredients in a large punch bowl; stir to mix well. Serves 20.

Bananas, apples and tomatoes ripen quickly if placed overnight in a brown paper bag.

Dilly Macaroni Salad

Debra Ivie
Prineville, OR

I often make this for my husband to take to his Friday night poker game. Everyone there really likes it, especially our friend Jeremy and our grandson Nic. I have to admit...it's one of my favorites too!

2 12-oz. pkgs. elbow macaroni,
    uncooked
10 to 12 eggs, hard-boiled,
    peeled and diced
6 to 7 dill pickle spears, diced
1/2 to 1 c. dill pickle juice
15-oz. can sliced black olives,
    drained

1-1/2 c. mayonnaise
1/3 c. mustard
5 T. dill weed
2 T. dried, minced onion
1 T. garlic salt
2 t. seasoned salt
salt and pepper to taste

Cook macaroni according to package directions; drain and rinse with cold water. Combine macaroni and remaining ingredients in a large bowl; sauce will be thin. Cover and refrigerate for at least 4 hours. Stir again before serving. Makes 20 to 25 servings.

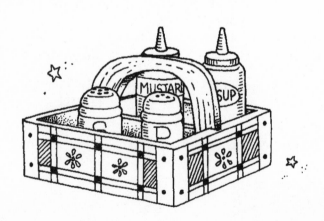

Make a quick condiment kit for your next backyard barbecue.
Just place salt, pepper, mustard, catsup, flatware and napkins
in an empty cardboard pop carrier...so easy!

Party Pepperoni Bread

Janet Myers
Reading, PA

Slices of this savory bread get snatched up so quickly at the buffet table, you'd better grab some first! Zesty Italian flavors rolled in a warm and crusty loaf of bread...what more could you ask for?

1/2 t. shortening
1-lb. loaf frozen bread dough
3/4 t. dried parsley

3/4 t. dried oregano
4-oz. pkg. sliced pepperoni
2 c. shredded mozzarella cheese

Spread shortening over frozen bread dough. Let dough thaw and rise according to package directions. Press dough onto a lightly greased 15"x10" jelly-roll pan. Sprinkle herbs over dough. Top with pepperoni slices, leaving a 1/4-inch border around the edge; sprinkle with mozzarella cheese. Roll up dough, starting at a long edge; pinch seams together to seal. Place seam-side down on a lightly greased baking sheet. Poke multiple holes in bread with a knife tip to vent. Bake at 350 degrees for 20 to 25 minutes, until golden. Let stand 5 minutes before slicing. Makes 20 servings.

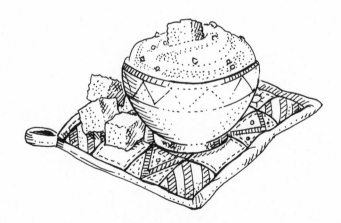

Why not try Party Pepperoni Bread with a different Italian deli meat? There's plenty to choose from...salami, soppresatta, prosciutto, capicola, mortadella...and all of them are so tasty!

Turtle Pie

Stephanie Corsaro
Hurricane, WV

A quick & easy favorite for any occasion.

1/2 c. brown sugar, packed
1 c. all-purpose flour
3/4 c. chopped nuts
1/2 c. butter, melted

14-oz. jar caramel topping,
  divided
2 qts. vanilla ice cream

In a bowl, mix together brown sugar, flour, nuts and butter. Spread mixture on a lightly greased baking sheet; bake at 400 degrees for 10 minutes, or until crisp. Cool completely. Crumble crust and transfer to a 13"x9" baking pan, reserving 1/4 cup for topping. Pour half the jar of caramel over crumbled crust. Spread ice cream over caramel. Drizzle with remaining caramel; sprinkle with reserved crust crumbles. Freeze for at least 2 hours before serving. Cut into squares. Serves 24.

Old-Fashioned Lemonade

Vickie

There's nothing like a big glass of ice-cold lemonade
on a hot day...so delightful!

1 c. fresh lemon juice
3/4 to 1 c. sugar

4 c. cold water
Garnish: ice cubes, lemon slices

Combine juice and sugar in a pitcher; mix until sugar is dissolved. Stir in water. If too tart, add more sugar to taste. Serve lemonade over ice; garnish drinking glasses with lemon slices. Makes about 5 cups.

STADIUM-SIZED
Recipes for a Crowd

Bubbly Tomato Bake for a Crowd

Darlene Bailis
Massillon, OH

This recipe is so popular at family picnics, I now have to double it whenever I bring it anywhere. Fresh tomatoes topped with golden cheese...this makes a savory baked dish brimming with delicious summer flavor!

12 southern-style refrigerated
   biscuits
5 to 6 tomatoes, thinly sliced
1/4 c. fresh basil, chopped
salt and pepper to taste

1/4 c. plus 2 T. green onions,
   sliced
1-1/4 c. mayonnaise
8-oz. pkg. shredded Monterey
   Jack cheese

Place biscuits in a lightly greased 13"x9" baking pan. Flatten biscuits and pinch seams together to seal. Arrange tomatoes on top of dough. Sprinkle with basil, salt and pepper; top with green onions. In a bowl, mix together mayonnaise and cheese. Spoon mayonnaise mixture evenly over all, completely covering tomatoes. Bake, uncovered, at 425 degrees for 12 to 15 minutes, or until heated through and crust is golden. Let stand 15 minutes before cutting into squares. Serves 12 to 16.

Look for heirloom fruits & vegetables at farmers' markets... varieties that Grandma & Grandpa may have grown in their garden. These fruits and veggies look so unique and their time-tested flavor can't be beat!

Polish Sauerkraut & Kielbasa

Joyce Jonker
Kalkaska, MI

This classic comfort dish really hits the spot on a chilly fall evening. A big bowl of this is sure to keep you warm all throughout the football game!

1/2 lb. bacon, diced
2 onions, diced
1 head cabbage, chopped
2 15-oz. cans chicken broth
32-oz. jar sauerkraut

Optional: brown sugar to taste
salt and pepper to taste
2 14-oz. Kielbasa sausage rings,
    sliced 1/2-inch thick

In a large stockpot over medium heat, cook bacon until crisp. Drain, reserving one tablespoon drippings in the stockpot. Sauté onions in drippings until translucent. Add cabbage and broth to stockpot. Cook, stirring often, until cabbage cooks down. Stir in sauerkraut with juice and bacon. If too tart, add brown sugar to taste. Season with salt and pepper. Stir in Kielbasa. Cook, stirring occasionally, until Kielbasa is heated through. Serves 12 to 15.

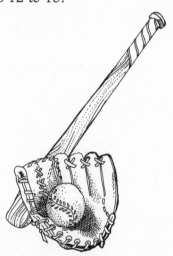

Life's like a ballgame. You gotta take a swing
at whatever comes along before you wake up
and find it's the ninth inning.

–Martin Goldsmith

INDEX

Appetizers & Snacks

Amanda's Spicy Sweet Potato Fries, 41
Bacon-Wrapped Water Chestnuts, 200
Beer-Battered Fried Veggies, 61
Cajun Boiled Peanuts, 46
Chase & Brady's Bacon Puffs, 40
Crab & Shrimp Poppers, 50
Deluxe Texas Nachos, 36
Fast & Easy Meatballs, 74
Fried Dill Pickles, 42
Game-Time TV Mix, 193
Game-Day Dim Sum, 199
Game-Day Meatballs, 205
Game-Day Piggies, 57
Grandma Hovey's Party Meatballs, 62
Grandma's Polish "Pizza," 66
Healthy Jalapeño Poppers, 55
Hearty Slow-Cooker Nachos, 52
Herbed Deviled Eggs, 44
Jalapeño Pepper Poppers, 186
Little Sugar Piggies, 200
Loaded Deviled Eggs, 43
Mexican Egg Rolls, 59
Nutty Cheese-Stuffed Celery, 73
Party Cocktail Sausages, 40
Party Pepperoni Bread, 215
Party Pizza Bites, 69
Pepperoni Bread, 53
Pepperoni Roll-ups, 67
Pizza Muffins, 54
Ragin' Cajun Mozzarella Sticks, 63
Sausage Pizza-Stuffed Mushrooms, 210
Slow-Cooker Buffalo Chicken
    Nachos, 37
Spicy BBQ Chicken Wings, 51
Stuffed Pepperoncini, 74
Sweet Chipotle Pretzels, 46
The Best Bruschetta, 68
Touchdown Toss, 45
Uncle Bruce's Snack Mix, 45

Beverages

Frosty Banana Punch, 213
Iced Coffee Punch, 192
Margarita Punch, 213
Old-Fashioned Lemonade, 216

Breakfast & Brunch

Baked Denver Omelet, 16
Beer Bread Pancakes, 15
Blueberry Pancake Cake, 24
Bunch for Brunch Eggs, 207
Busy-Morning Breakfast Pizza, 23
Canadian Bacon Waffles, 31
Cannoli French Toast, 21
Cheesy Chicken Omelet, 10
Chocolate Chip Banana Pancakes, 17
Easy Huevos Rancheros Casserole, 206
Fresh Spinach Quiche, 19
Goal-Line Sausage Casserole, 6
Good Morning Biscuits & Gravy, 33
Gretta's Ham, Potato & Cheddar
    Quiche, 29
Ham & Corn Griddle Cakes, 14
Jumbo Cinnamon Rolls, 18
Line-Drive Doughnuts, 22
Mama's Camping Burritos, 12
Maple Monkey Bread, 27
Michelle's Chicken Strata, 185
Michigan Game-Day Oatmeal, 16
Migas, 11
Mother's Crispy Crumb Eggs, 25
Mrs. V's Southwest Quiche, 7
Muffin-Tin Breakfast Quiche, 24
No-Bake Fruit & Nut Cereal Bars, 32
Peanut Butter Pancake Syrup, 8
Pumpkin Pancakes & Waffles, 8
Pumpkin-Caramel Doughnut Holes, 34
Reuben Quiche, 9
Salami & Egg Sandwiches, 23
Sausage & Grits Casserole, 20
Savory Sausage Squares, 26
Skillet Crumb Cake, 13
Slow-Cooker Piggies in Eggs, 13
Sugared Bacon, 31
Sunday Bacon & Cheese Pull-Apart, 28
Yummy Blueberry Coffee Cake, 30

Cakes & Pies

77 Carrot Cake, 165
All-Star Boston Cream Pie, 160
Apple Pie Cake, 164
Candy Bar Pie, 176

INDEX

Citrus Soda Cake, 166
Cookie Cupcakes, 174
Derby Day Chocolate Pecan Pie, 148
Devil's Food Cake, 156
Grandmother's Icebox Cake, 180
Granny Ruby's Fried Pies, 176
Hoosier Cake, 149
Key Lime Pound Cake, 161
Lemonade Pie, 164
Man-on-the-Moon Cake, 175
Mini Cheesecakes, 190
Mini Pie Bites, 191
Mom's Wacky Cake, 201
No-Bake Apple Pie, 152
Peanut Butter Cheesecake, 181
Peanut Butter Fudge Pie, 159
Turtle Pie, 216

Cookies, Brownies & Bars

Brownie-Stuffed Chocolate Chip
  Cookies, 173
Cocoa Snickerdoodles, 155
Coconut Crunch Pretzel Bars, 212
Coconutty Macaroons, 172
Jake's Magic Square Bars, 171
Judy's Salty-Sweet Peanut Cookies, 169
Malted Milk Squares, 170
Minty Chocolate Brownies, 151
No-Bake Butterscotch Bars, 181
Pig-Out Cookies, 168
S'mores Bars, 167
Skillet Cookies, 178
Spicy-Hot Brownies, 150
Strawberry-Lemon Shortbread Bars, 163
Tumbleweeds, 172
World's Best Cookies, 177

Desserts

Banana Pudding Fudge, 158
Caramel Bananas, 158
Chipotle Caramels, 157
Five Pounds of Fudge, 211
Frozen Pineapple Slush, 162
Goofer Balls, 154
Homemade Vanilla Ice Cream, 179
Ice Cream Sandwich Dessert, 202
Margarita Watermelon Slices, 162
Marshmallow Treats-on-a-Stick, 167

Old-Fashioned Caramel Corn, 153
Ooey-Gooey Popcorn, 153
Peanutty Ice Cream Roll, 179
Pumpkin Torte, 182

Dips, Spreads & Sauces

10-Layer Taco Dip, 194
3-Cheese Beer Fondue, 56
4-H Michigan Sauce, 103
Awesome Dip, 65
Black Bean Salsa, 39
Buetow's Mini Cheese Balls, 189
Caramelized Onion Dip, 71
Charlie's Steakhouse Cheese Spread, 48
Chili con Queso, 209
Coney Dog Sauce, 103
Creamy Crabby Dip, 50
Easy Cheesy Bean Dip, 38
Floorboard Bean Dip, 204
Gridiron Guacamole, 60
Hot Hamburger Dip, 65
Jalapeño Popper Dip, 209
Mexican Pizza Dip, 187
Mixed-Up Olive Dip, 49
Nan's Chipped Beef & Pimento Cheese
  Ball, 203
Pecan-Crusted Salmon Ball, 72
Pico de Gallo, 60
Pimento Cheese Spread, 64
Slow-Cooker Spinach & Artichoke
  Dip, 47
Spinach & Artichoke Dip, 64
Straight From Buffalo Chicken
  Wing Dip, 58
Verne's East Texas Salsa, 70

Mains

3-Cheese Baked Spaghetti, 145
Arroz con Pollo, 129
Baked Cheesy Chicken Penne, 208
Baked Sweet-and-Sour Chicken, 116
Buffalo Chicken Stromboli, 132
Chicken Wings 4 Ways, 125
Easy Stuffed Shells for a Crowd, 146
Enchilada Lasagna, 131
Friday Night Pizza, 119
Game-Day Garden Pizza, 135
Heavenly Hot Dogs, 111

INDEX

Hot Dog Boats, 142
Jane's Barbecue Wings, 126
Karolina's Oven-Fried Chicken, 136
Kim's Crustless Pizza, 134
Mitchell's Wonderful Brisket, 122
Old-Fashioned Corn Dogs, 112
Onside Kickin' Chicken Kabobs, 124
Pittsburgh Pigskin Pierogies, 126
Polish Sauerkraut & Kielbasa, 218
Sesame Pork Ribs, 117
Slow-Cooker Beef & Bean Burritos, 197
Smoky Stuffed Peppers, 128
Super Bowl Brisket, 137
Tailgate Roast, 137
Tasty Fajitas, 130
Tipsy Pork Chops, 144
Tostada Pizza, 141

Salads

All-Season Coleslaw, 99
Caprese Pasta Salad, 93
Carolina-Style Slaw Dressing, 99
Crunchy Oriental Coleslaw, 78
Dilly Macaroni Salad, 214
Grammy's Trio Pasta, 188
Mashed Potato Salad, 78
Mom's Spaghetti Salad, 85
Norma's Fumi Salad, 198
Redskin Potato Salad, 79
Simple Pepper Slaw, 85
Spicy Cajun Potato Salad, 100
Sweet & Salty Pretzel Salad, 90
Zesty Chicken Pasta Salad, 89

Sandwiches

Apple-Chicken Salad Sandwich, 97
Bar-B-Q Sliders, 109
Cakewich, 92
Chicken-Bacon Quesadilla, 86
Colossal Italian Sandwich, 91
Easy French Dip Sandwiches, 205
German Spiessbraten, 94
Hole-In-One Pimento-Cheese
    Sandwiches, 76
Italian Beef Dip Sandwiches, 105
Junkyard Joes, 133
Marvelous Meatball Subs, 118

Pocket Sammies, 97
Prosciutto Burgers, 121
Pulled Pork Sammies, 76
Race-Day Shredded Pork, 108
Red Devil Franks, 84
Reuben Roll, 98
Slow-Cooker Cheesesteak
    Sandwiches, 80
Spicy Italian Sausage Subs, 83
Teriyaki Burgers, 115
Turkey & Potato Hand Pies, 132
Upper Peninsula Pasties, 127

Sides

Bacon-Wrapped Corn on the Cob, 110
Bubbly Tomato Bake for a Crowd, 217
Creamy Bacon Corn-Fetti, 110
Curtis's Cheesy Creamy Twice-Baked
    Potatoes, 114
Fishing Buddies Hushpuppies, 143
Jo Jo Potatoes, 143
Judi's Green Chili & Cheddar Bread, 139
Mexican Cornbread, 140
Nana's Baked Beans, 138
Spanish Rice in a Snap, 120
Super-Easy Mac & Cheese, 120
Texas Cowboy Beans, 123
Traci's Easy Hashbrown Casserole, 189
Walter's Smoky Potatoes, 113

Soups

6-Pack Texas Stew, 81
Bacon Potato Chowder, 195
Beer-Cheese Soup, 77
Debbie's Clam Chowder for a
    Crowd, 184
Ditalini Nicoline Soup, 93
Kick-It-Right Chili, 102
Michelle's Spicy Vegetarian Chili, 87
Sensational Sausage & Kale Soup, 106
South Carolina Gumbo, 101
Spicy Italian Sausage Stew, 104
The Best Chicken & Corn Chowder, 96
Unstuffed Green Pepper Soup, 82
Vegetable Beef Soup for 50, 196
White Cheddar-Ale Soup, 95
White Chicken Chili, 88

Have a taste for more?

We created our official Circle of Friends so we could
fill everyone in on the latest scoop at once.
Visit us online to join in the fun and discover free
recipes, exclusive giveaways and much more!

www.gooseberrypatch.com

Email Club

Call us toll-free at 1·800·854·6673

U.S. to Canadian recipe equivalents

Volume Measurements

1/4 teaspoon	1 mL
1/2 teaspoon	2 mL
1 teaspoon	5 mL
1 tablespoon = 3 teaspoons	15 mL
2 tablespoons = 1 fluid ounce	30 mL
1/4 cup	60 mL
1/3 cup	75 mL
1/2 cup = 4 fluid ounces	125 mL
1 cup = 8 fluid ounces	250 mL
2 cups = 1 pint =16 fluid ounces	500 mL
4 cups = 1 quart	1 L

Weights

1 ounce	30 g
4 ounces	120 g
8 ounces	225 g
16 ounces = 1 pound	450 g

Oven Temperatures

300° F	150° C
325° F	160° C
350° F	180° C
375° F	190° C
400° F	200° C
450° F	230° C

Baking Pan Sizes

Square

8x8x2 inches	2 L = 20x20x5 cm
9x9x2 inches	2.5 L = 23x23x5 cm

Rectangular

13x9x2 inches	3.5 L = 33x23x5 cm

Loaf

9x5x3 inches	2 L = 23x13x7 cm

Round

8x1-1/2 inches	1.2 L = 20x4 cm
9x1-1/2 inches	1.5 L = 23x4 cm

YOUR recipe could appear in our next cookbook!

Share your tried & true family favorites with us instantly at

www.gooseberrypatch.com

If you'd rather jot 'em down by hand, just mail this form to...

Gooseberry Patch • Cookbooks – Call for Recipes
2500 Farmers Dr., #110 • Columbus, OH 43235

If your recipe is selected for a book, you'll receive a FREE copy!

Please share only your original recipes or those that you have made your own over the years.

Recipe Name:

Number of Servings:

Any fond memories about this recipe? Special touches you like to add
or handy shortcuts?

Ingredients (include specific measurements):

Instructions (continue on back if needed):

Special Code: **cookbookspage**

Over ➤

Extra space for recipe if needed:

Tell us about yourself...

Your complete contact information is needed so that we can send you your FREE cookbook, if your recipe is published. Phone numbers and email addresses are kept private and will only be used if we have questions about your recipe.

Name:

Address:

City: State: Zip:

Email:

Daytime Phone:

Thank you! Vickie & Jo Ann